NEHEMIAH

Experiencing the Good Hand of God

JOHN
MACARTHUR

NEHEMIAH
MACARTHUR BIBLE STUDIES

Cover Art by The Puckett Group.
Interior design and composition by Design Corps, Batavia, IL.

Produced with the assistance of the Livingstone Corporation. Project staff
include Dave Veerman, Christopher D. Hudson, and Amber Rae.

Project editor: Len Woods

ISBN-13: 978-0-8499-5550-1

09 QW 19

Nehemiah

Table of Contents

THE BOOK OF NEHEMIAH

Introduction

Nehemiah ("Yahweh comforts") is a famous cup-bearer, who never appears in Scripture outside of this book. As with the books of Ezra and Esther, named after his contemporaries, the book recounts selected events of his leadership and was titled after him. Both the Septuagint (LXX) —a Greek translation of the Old Testament—and the Latin Vulgate named this book "Second Ezra." Even though the two books of Ezra and Nehemiah are separate in most English Bibles, they may have once been joined together in a single unit as currently in the Hebrew texts. New Testament writers do not quote Nehemiah.

Author and Date

Though much of this book was clearly drawn from Nehemiah's personal diaries and written from his first person perspective (1:1–7:5; 12:27–43; 13:4–31), both Jewish and Christian traditions recognize Ezra as the author. This is based on external evidence that Ezra and Nehemiah were originally one book, as reflected in the LXX and Vulgate; it is also based on internal evidence such as the recurrent "hand of the LORD" theme that dominates both Ezra and Nehemiah, and the author's role as a priest-scribe. As a scribe, he had access to the royal archives of Persia, which accounts for the myriad of administrative documents found recorded in the two books, especially in the Book of Ezra. Very few people would have been allowed access to the royal archives of the Persian Empire, but Ezra proved to be the exception (see Ezra 1:2–4; 4:9–22; 5:7–17; 6:3–12).

The events in Nehemiah 1 commence late in the year 446 B.C., the twentith year of the Persian king, Artaxerxes (464–423 B.C.). The book follows chronologically from Nehemiah's first term as governor of Jerusalem about 445–433 B.C. (Neh. 1–12) to his second term, possibly beginning about 424 B.C. (Neh. 13). Nehemiah was written by Ezra sometime during or after Nehemiah's second term, but no later than 400 B.C.

Background and Setting

True to God's promise of judgment, He brought the Assyrians and Babylonians to deliver His chastisement upon wayward Judah and Israel. In 722 B.C. the Assyrians deported the ten northern tribes and scattered them all over the then known world (2 Kings 17). Several centuries later, about 605–586 B.C., God used the Babylonians to sack, destroy, and nearly depopulate Jerusalem (2 Kings 25) because Judah had persisted in her unfaithfulness to the covenant. God chastened His people with 70 years of captivity in Babylon (Jer. 25:11).

During the Jews' captivity, world empire leadership changed hands from the Babylonians to the Persians (about 539 B.C.; Dan. 5), after which Daniel received most of his prophetic revelation (see Dan. 6, 9–12). The book of Ezra begins with the decree of Cyrus, a Persian king, to return God's people to Jerusalem to rebuild God's house (about 539 B.C.), and chronicles the reestablishment of Judah's national calendar of feasts and sacrifices. Zerubbabel and Joshua led the first return (Ezra 1–6) and rebuilt the temple. Esther gives a glimpse of the Jews left in Persia (about 483–473 B.C.) when Haman attempted to eliminate the Jewish race. Ezra 7–10 recounts the second return led by Ezra in 458 B.C. Nehemiah chronicles the third return to rebuild the wall around Jerusalem (about 445 B.C.).

At that time in Judah's history, the Persian Empire dominated the entire Near Eastern world. Its administration of Judah, although carried out with a loose hand, was mindful of disruptions or any signs of rebellion from its vassals. Rebuilding the walls of conquered cities posed the most glaring threat to the Persian central administration. Only a close confidant of the king himself could be trusted for such an operation. At the most critical juncture in Judah's revitalization, God raised up Nehemiah to exercise one of the most trusted roles in the empire, that of the king's cup-bearer and confidant. Life under the Persian king Artaxerxes (about 464–423 B.C.) had its advantages for Nehemiah. Much like Joseph, Esther, and Daniel, he had attained a significant role in the palace which then ruled the ancient world, a position from which God could use him to lead the rebuilding of Jerusalem's walls in spite of its implications for Persian control of that city.

Several other historical notes are of interest. First, Daniel's prophetic 70 weeks began with the decree issued by Artaxerxes in 445 B.C. to rebuild the city. (see chaps. 1, 2; see Dan. 9:24–26). Second, the Elephantine papyri (Egyptian documents), dated to the late 5th century B.C., support the account of Nehemiah by mentioning Sanballat the governor of Samaria (2:19), Jehohanan (6:18; 12:23), and Nehemiah's being replaced as governor of Jerusalem by Bigvai (about 410 B.C.; Neh. 10:16). Finally, Nehemiah and Malachi represent the last of the Old Testament canonical writings, both in terms of the time the events occurred (Mal. 1–4; Neh. 13) and the time when they were recorded by Ezra. Thus the next messages from God for Israel do not come until over 400 years of silence had passed, after which the births of John the Baptist and Jesus Christ were announced (Matt. 1; Luke 1, 2).

With the full Old Testament revelation of Israel's history prior to Christ's incarnation being completed, the Jews had not yet experienced the fullness of God's various covenants and promises to them. While there was a Jewish remnant, as promised to Abraham (see Gen. 15:5), it does not appear to be even as large as at the time of the Exodus (Num. 1:46). The Jews neither possessed the Land (Gen. 15:7), nor did they rule as a sovereign nation (Gen. 12:2). The Davidic throne was unoccupied (see 2 Sam. 7:16), although the High Priest was of the line of Eleazar and Phinehas (see Num. 25:10–13). God's promise to consummate the New Covenant of redemption awaited the birth, crucifixion, and resurrection of Messiah (see Heb. 7–10).

Historical and Theological Themes

Careful attention to the reading of God's Word in order to perform His will is a constant theme. The spiritual revival came in response to Ezra's reading of "the Book of the Law of Moses" (8:1). After the reading, Ezra and some of the priests carefully explained its meaning to the people in attendance (8:8). The next day, Ezra met with some of the fathers of the households, the priests, and Levites, "in order to understand the words of the Law" (8:13). The sacrificial system was carried on with careful attention to perform it "as it is written in the Law" (10:34, 36). So deep was their concern to abide by God's revealed will that they took "a curse and an oath to walk in God's Law" (10:29). When the marriage reforms were carried out, they acted in accordance with that which "they read from the Book of Moses" (13:1).

A second major theme, the obedience of Nehemiah, is explicitly referred to throughout the book, because the book is based on the memoirs or first-person accounts of Nehemiah. God worked through the obedience of Nehemiah; however, He also worked through the wrongly motivated, wicked hearts of His enemies. Nehemiah's enemies failed, not so much as a result of the success of Nehemiah's strategies, but because "God had brought their plot to nothing" (4:15). God used the opposition of Judah's enemies to drive His people to their knees in the same way that He used the favor of Cyrus to return His people to the Land, to fund their building project, and to protect the reconstruction of Jerusalem's walls. Not surprisingly, Nehemiah acknowledged the true motive of his strategy to repopulate Jerusalem: "My God put it into my heart" (7:5). It was He who accomplished it.

Another theme in Nehemiah, as in Ezra, is opposition. Judah's enemies started rumors that God's people had revolted against Persia. The goal was to intimidate Judah into forestalling reconstruction of the walls. In spite of opposition from without and heartbreaking corruption and dissension from within, Judah completed the walls of Jerusalem in only 52 days (6:15), experienced revival after the reading of the law by Ezra (8:1), and celebrated the Feast of Tabernacles (8:14; about 445 B.C.).

The book's detailed insight into the personal thoughts, motives, and disappointments of Nehemiah makes it easy for the reader to primarily identify with him, rather than "the sovereign hand of God" theme and the primary message of His control and intervention into the affairs of His people and their enemies. But the exemplary behavior of the famous cupbearer is eclipsed by God, who orchestrated the reconstruction of the walls in spite of much opposition and many setbacks; the "good hand of God" theme carries through the book of Nehemiah (1:10; 2:8, 18).

Interpretive Challenges

First, much of Nehemiah is explained in relationship to Jerusalem's gates (see chapters 2, 3, 8, 12). Second, the reader must recognize that the time line of chapters 1–12 encompassed about one year (445 B.C.), followed by a long gap of time (over 20 years) after chapter 12 and before chapter 13. Finally, it must be recognized that Nehemiah actually served two governorships in Jerusalem, the first from 445 to 433 B.C. (see 5:14; 13:6) and the second beginning possibly in 424 B.C. and extending to no longer than 410 B.C.

OUTLINE

I. Nehemiah's First Term as Governor (1:1–12:47)
    A. Nehemiah's Return and Reconstruction (1:1–7:73a)
        1. Nehemiah goes to Jerusalem (1:1–2:20)
        2. Nehemiah and the people rebuild the walls (3:1–7:3)
        3. Nehemiah recalls the first return under Zerubbabel (7:4–73a)
    B. Ezra's Revival and Renewal (7:73b–10:39)
        1. Ezra expounds the law (7:73b–8:12)
        2. The people worship and repent (8:13–9:37)
        3. Ezra and the priests renew the covenant (9:38–10:39)
    C. Nehemiah's Resettlement and Rejoicing (11:1–12:47)
        1. Jerusalem is resettled (11:1–12:26)
        2. The people dedicate the walls (12:27–47)
II. Nehemiah's Second Term as Governor (13:1–31)

A Man with a Burden

Opening Thought

1) About what issues or problems do you feel most passionate? Why do you think these things concern you more than other equally troubling situations?

_____

_____

_____

2) How would you rate your prayer life just now (1 = "awful"; 10 = "awesome"). When was your prayer life the strongest? Why?

_____

_____

_____

3) When you hear bad news about people you care about, what is your typical reaction/response? Why?

_____

_____

_____

4) If you were facing a time of trial or hardship, what would you want your friends and loved ones to do for you?

_____

_____

_____

Background of the Passage

The book of Nehemiah is a wonderful primer for anyone who faces a daunting situation and needs to be reminded that deep trust in and unflinching obedience to Almighty God can result in the accomplishment of the "impossible." Nehemiah is a book about dreaming big dreams, about solving monumental problems, about the power of prayer, about standing strong in the face of harsh opposition, and about motivating people and leading groups to do great works for a great God.

The historical context is important in understanding the story of Nehemiah. Following the death of Solomon in 931 B.C., Israel split into two entities. The northern kingdom, comprised of ten tribes, took the name Israel. The southern kingdom became known as Judah (which was the name of the larger of the two remaining tribes). A long history of disobedience and idolatry resulted in the northern kingdom's being conquered by Assyria in 722 B.C. In 605 B.C. the southern kingdom suffered a similar fate at the hands of the Babylonians. As per the unheeded words of the prophets, there followed a 70-year period of captivity or exile for the people of God. But with the rise of the Medo-Persian Empire, and the subsequent defeat of the Babylonians, the Jews were granted permission by Cyrus to return to their homeland. They did so under several leaders over a period of about 100 years (Zerubbabel in 538, Ezra in 458, and Nehemiah in 445).

Nehemiah was neither a priest nor a prophet. He was a layman in a unique and remarkable position of influence. As cupbearer to King Artaxerxes of Persia, Nehemiah enjoyed a life of privilege and access. He was a trusted civil servant-likely present during high-level meetings and probably advising the most powerful man on earth on matters of state.

What will happen when this faithful man of God hears that his countrymen back in Jerusalem are facing ridicule and danger because the city's walls and gates are in shambles? How will Nehemiah's faith manifest itself in a way that brings glory to God? Those are the issues and situations in Nehemiah 1.

Bible Passage

Read 1:1–11, noting the key words and definitions to the right of the passage.

Nehemiah 1:1–11:

¹ *The words of Nehemiah the son of Hachaliah. It came to pass in the month of Chislev, in the twentieth year, as I was in Shushan the citadel,*

² *that Hanani one of my brethren came with men from Judah; and I asked them concerning the Jews who had escaped, who had survived the captivity, and concerning Jerusalem.*

³ *And they said to me, "The survivors who are left from the captivity in the province are there in great distress and reproach. The wall of Jerusalem is also broken down, and its gates are burned with fire."*

⁴ *So it was, when I heard these words, that I sat down and wept, and mourned for many days; I was fasting and praying before the God of heaven.*

⁵ *And I said: "I pray, LORD God of heaven, O great and awesome God, You who keep Your covenant and mercy with those who love You and observe Your commandments,*

⁶ *"please let Your ear be attentive and Your eyes open, that You may hear the prayer of Your servant which I pray before You now, day and night, for the children of Israel Your servants, and confess the sins of the children of Israel which we have sinned against You. Both my father's house and I have sinned.*

⁷ *"We have acted very corruptly against You, and have not kept the commandments, the statutes, nor the ordinances which You commanded Your servant Moses.*

⁸ *"Remember, I pray, the word that You commanded Your servant Moses, saying, 'If you are unfaithful, I will scatter you among the nations;*

⁹ *'but if you return to Me, and keep My commandments and do them, though some of you were cast out to the farthest part of the heavens, yet I will gather them from there, and bring them to*

The words of Nehemiah (v. 1) —The personal records of this famous royal cupbearer, whose name means "Yahweh comforts" (see 3:16; 7:7; 8:9; 10:1; 12:26, 47), contribute greatly to this book. Unlike Esther and Mordecai, named after Mesopotamian deities Ishtar and Marduk, Nehemiah was given a Hebrew name.

Hachaliah (v. 1)—Nehemiah's father is mentioned again in Nehemiah 10:1, but nowhere else in the Old Testament.

Chislev (v. 1)—This is in November/December 446 B.C., four months before Nisan (Mar./Apr.), when Nehemiah came before the king to get permission to go to Jerusalem (2:1).

twentieth year (v. 1)—the twentieth year (about 446/445 B.C.) in the reign of Persian king Artaxerxes (about 464–423 B.C.; see 2:1)

Shushan (v. 1)—Also known as Susa, this city was situated east of Babylon, about one hundred fifty miles north of the Persian Gulf. Shushan was one of the Medo-Persian strongholds, a wintering city for many officials, and the setting of Esther.

Hanani (v. 2—Apparently a sibling of Nehemiah (see 7:2), he had gone to Jerusalem in the second return under Ezra's leadership (about 458 B.C.).

Jews . . . Jerusalem (v. 2)— Nehemiah was deeply concerned about the people and the city, especially during the previous thirteen years, since the second return under Ezra (458 B.C.).

wall of Jerusalem . . . gates (v. 3)—The opposition had successfully thwarted the Jews' attempts to reestablish Jerusalem

9

the place which I have chosen as a dwelling for My name.'

10 "Now these are Your servants and Your people, whom You have redeemed by Your great power, and by Your strong hand.

11 "O Lord, I pray, please let Your ear be attentive to the prayer of Your servant, and to the prayer of Your servants who desire to fear Your name; and let Your servant prosper this day, I pray, and grant him mercy in the sight of this man." For I was the king's cupbearer.

as a distinctively Jewish city capable of withstanding its enemies' assaults, which could possibly lead to another destruction of the newly rebuilt temple (about 516B.C.; see Ezra 4:7–23).

sat down and wept, and mourned for many days (v. 4) —Although Nehemiah was neither a prophet nor a priest, he had a deep sense of Jerusalem's significance to God and was greatly distressed that affairs there had not advanced the cause and glory of God.

"I pray, LORD God of heaven..." (v. 5)—This prayer represents one of the Scripture's most moving confessions and intercessions before God (see Dan. 9:4–19; Ezra 9:6–15).

keep Your covenant and mercy with those who love You (v. 5)—After seventy years of captivity in Babylon, God kept His promise to restore His people to the Promised Land. The promise appeared to be failing, and Nehemiah appealed to God's character and covenant as the basis by which He must intervene and accomplish His pledges to His people.

we have sinned against You (v. 6)—Nehemiah may have believed that the sins of the returnees (see Ezra 9,10) had prompted God to change His mind and withhold His favor from the Jews.

commandments . . . statutes . . . ordinances (v. 7) —those recorded in Exodus, Leviticus, Numbers, and Deuteronomy

Remember (v. 8)—not a reminder to God as if He had forgotten, but a plea to activate His Word

the word . . . Moses (vv. 8, 9)—This represents a summary of various Mosaic writings.

redeemed by Your great power, and by Your strong hand (v. 10)—His allusion to the Exodus redemption recalled the faithful and strong hand of God, which had brought Israel out of bondage once before. The statement grounded Nehemiah's confidence in God's power as the basis of his appeal for a second deliverance that will be as successful as the first.

who desire to fear Your name (v. 11)—Nehemiah alluded to the fact that Israel was the place that God had chosen for His name to dwell (1:9); the people desired to fear His name and, thus, were praying for God's intervention.

in the sight of this man (v. 11)—The reference to King Artaxerxes anticipated the discussion in 2:1–8.

the king's cupbearer (v. 11)—As an escort of the monarch at meals, the cupbearer had a unique opportunity to petition the king. Not only did the king owe him his life since the cupbearer tested all the king's beverages for possible poison, thus putting his own life at risk, but he also became a close confidant. God sovereignly used this relationship between a Gentile and Jew to deliver His people, as He did with Joseph, Daniel, Esther, and Mordecai.

Understanding the Text

5) Why did Nehemiah question Hanani about Jerusalem?

_____

_____

_____

_____

_____

6) How did Nehemiah respond/react to the update from his homeland? Why?

_____

_____

_____

_____

_____

7) How did Nehemiah describe God in his prayer?

_____

_____

_____

_____

(verses to consider: 2 Samuel 7:18–29; 1 Kings 8:22–53)

8) What was the content of Nehemiah's prayer? What promises of God did he mention? How did he describe the people of God?

_____

_____

_____

_____

(verses to consider: Ezra 9:6–15; Dan. 9:4–19)

9) Why does Nehemiah almost "off-handedly" mention that he was cup-bearer to the king? What is significant about this?

_____

_____

_____

_____

_____

_____

Cross Reference

Read Ezra 4:7–24.

> ⁷ *In the days of Artaxerxes also, Bishlam, Mithredath, Tabel, and the rest of their companions wrote to Artaxerxes king of Persia; and the letter was written in Aramaic script, and translated into the Aramaic language.*

⁸ Rehum the commander and Shimshai the scribe wrote a letter against Jerusalem to King Artaxerxes in this fashion:

⁹ From Rehum the commander, Shimshai the scribe, and the rest of their companions—representatives of the Dinaites, the Apharsathchites, the Tarpelites, the people of Persia and Erech and Babylon and Shushan, the Dehavites, the Elamites,

¹⁰ and the rest of the nations whom the great and noble Osnapper took captive and settled in the cities of Samaria and the remainder beyond the River—and so forth.

¹¹ (This is a copy of the letter that they sent him) To King Artaxerxes from your servants, the men of the region beyond the River, and so forth:

¹² Let it be known to the king that the Jews who came up from you have come to us at Jerusalem, and are building the rebellious and evil city, and are finishing its walls and repairing the foundations.

¹³ Let it now be known to the king that, if this city is built and the walls completed, they will not pay tax, tribute, or custom, and the king's treasury will be diminished.

¹⁴ Now because we receive support from the palace, it was not proper for us to see the king's dishonor; therefore we have sent and informed the king,

¹⁵ that search may be made in the book of the records of your fathers. And you will find in the book of the records and know that this city is a rebellious city, harmful to kings and provinces, and that they have incited sedition within the city in former times, for which cause this city was destroyed.

¹⁶ We inform the king that if this city is rebuilt and its walls are completed, the result will be that you will have no dominion beyond the River.

¹⁷ The king sent an answer: To Rehum the commander, to Shimshai the scribe, to the rest of their companions who dwell in Samaria, and to the remainder beyond the River: Peace, and so forth.

¹⁸ The letter which you sent to us has been clearly read before me.

¹⁹ And I gave the command, and a search has been made, and it was found that this city in former times has revolted against kings, and rebellion and sedition have been fostered in it.

²⁰ There have also been mighty kings over Jerusalem, who have ruled over all the region beyond the River; and tax, tribute, and custom were paid to them.

²¹ Now give the command to make these men cease, that this city may not be built until the command is given by me.

²² Take heed now that you do not fail to do this. Why should damage increase to the hurt of the kings?

²³ Now when the copy of King Artaxerxes' letter was read before Rehum, Shimshai the scribe, and their companions, they went up in haste to Jerusalem against the Jews, and by force of arms made them cease.

24 *Thus the work of the house of God which is at Jerusalem ceased, and it was discontinued until the second year of the reign of Darius king of Persia.*

Exploring the Meaning

10) How does this background passage from Ezra shed light on the events of Nehemiah 1?

_____

_____

_____

_____

_____

11) Read Micah 6:8. In what ways does Nehemiah meet the criteria of a man who walks with God?

_____

_____

_____

_____

_____

12) Read Acts 13:2 and 14:23. What is the purpose of fasting and when is it appropriate to do so?

_____

_____

_____

_____

(verses to consider: 1 Samuel 7:6; 2 Samuel 12:16–23; 2 Chronicles 20:3; Joel 1:14; 2:12)

Summing Up...

"A man full of faith toward God, and yielded to the Spirit's control, will be gracious toward others and manifest great spiritual power.

"Prayer is the spontaneous response of the believing heart to God. Those truly transformed by Jesus Christ find themselves lost in the wonder and joy of communion with Him. Prayer is as natural for the Christian as breathing."
—*John MacArthur*

Reflecting on the Text

13) What traits in Nehemiah's life (seen in chapter 1) do you need to emulate?

_____

_____

_____

_____

_____

14) What specific steps could you take this week to strengthen or improve your prayer life?

_____

_____

_____

_____

_____

15) How can you remind yourself this week to turn to God in prayer when you experience disappointment?

_____

_____

_____

_____

16) Write down the names of two people for whom you can intercede this week.

_____

_____

_____

_____

_____

Recording Your Thoughts

_____

_____

_____

_____

_____

_____

_____

_____

_____

For further study, see the following passages:

Deuteronomy 4:25–31	Deuteronomy 28:63–65	Deuteronomy 30:1–5
2 Kings 19:14–19	2 Chronicles 33:9–13	Esther 4:16
Matthew 6:16–18	Acts 4:23–31	

God's Man with God's Plan

Opening Thought

1) What kinds of situations make you nervous or fearful? Why?

_____

_____

2) If you could ask any favor of any person, whom would you ask? for what and why?

_____

_____

3) When it comes to planning and organizing, how would you describe yourself? Is it wrong for Christians to develop detailed plans for ministry ventures? Why or why not?

_____

_____

4) When criticized do you tend to:
- run away/withdraw?
- lash out/fight back?
- become insecure and inactive?
- other_____?

Why?

_____

_____

_____

Background of the Passage

Significant problems do not, typically, solve themselves. And rarely does God intervene in messy situations with dramatic and direct displays of supernatural power from on high. Most of the time God uses people—plain and ordinary (but also faithful, available, and obedient!) saints—to accomplish His will on the earth.

And yet even when it is obvious a situation needs to be addressed, and even when the evidence is clear that one is being summoned by God to serve as a catalyst for change, stepping forward in faith is difficult. Being an instrument of God requires uncommon courage as well as the creative application of all the resources one has been granted by God.

In chapter 1, we met Nehemiah, the Jewish cupbearer to the Persian king. We observed his deep concern for his countrymen. We caught a glimpse of his humble heart. We saw firsthand his deep-seated belief that God is the ultimate source of help, hope, and healing.

Now in chapter 2, we will have the privilege of watching what happens when God begins to answer Nehemiah's prayers. This meek servant of God finds great favor at the hands of King Artaxerxes. Not only is he granted permission to return to Jerusalem and reconstruct the walls, he is also supplied with ample resources, armed guards, letters of reference, and authority to act—as the newly appointed governor of Judah (see 5:14; 8:9; 10:1; 12:26).

After a journey of several months, Nehemiah arrives in Jerusalem. After three days' rest, he inspects the walls at night, so that he can formulate a plan of action.

Bible Passage

Read 2:1–20, noting the key words and definitions to the right of the passage.

Nehemiah 2:1–20:

¹ *And it came to pass in the month of Nisan, in the twentieth year of King Artaxerxes, when wine was before him, that I took the wine and gave it*

Nisan (v. 1)—March/April 545 B.C

when wine was before him (v. 1)—Since the act of tasting wine to ensure it was not dangerous to the king strengthened the

to the king. Now I had never been sad in his presence before.

²Therefore the king said to me, "Why is your face sad, since you are not sick? This is nothing but sorrow of heart." So I became dreadfully afraid,

³and said to the king, "May the king live forever! Why should my face not be sad, when the city, the place of my fathers' tombs, lies waste, and its gates are burned with fire?"

⁴Then the king said to me, "What do you request?" So I prayed to the God of heaven.

⁵And I said to the king, "If it pleases the king, and if your servant has found favor in your sight, I ask that you send me to Judah, to the city of my fathers' tombs, that I may rebuild it."

⁶Then the king said to me (the queen also sitting beside him), "How long will your journey be? And when will you return?" So it pleased the king to send me; and I set him a time.

⁷ Furthermore I said to the king, "If it pleases the king, let letters be given to me for the governors of the region beyond the River, that they must permit me to pass through till I come to Judah,

⁸ "and a letter to Asaph the keeper of the king's forest, that he must give me timber to make beams for the gates of the citadel which pertains to the temple, for the city wall, and for the house that I will occupy." And the king granted them to me according to the good hand of my God upon me.

⁹ Then I went to the governors in the region beyond the River, and gave them the king's letters. Now the king had sent captains of the army and horsemen with me.

¹⁰ When Sanballat the Horonite and Tobiah the Ammonite official heard of it, they were deeply disturbed that a man had come to seek the well-being of the children of Israel.

¹¹ So I came to Jerusalem and was there three days.

¹² Then I arose in the night, I and a few men with

trust between king and cupbearer, this was the appropriate time for Nehemiah to win Artaxerxes' attention and approval. Not surprisingly, kings often developed so much trust in their cupbearers that the latter became their counselors.

Now I had never been sad (v. 1)—Sadness was a dangerous emotion to express in the king's presence. The king wanted his subjects to be happy, since this reflected the well-being brought about by his administrative prowess.

dreadfully afraid (v. 2)—He feared that either his countenance, his explanation, or his request would anger the king and thus lead to his death.

tombs . . . gates (v. 3)—Nehemiah's deep concern and sadness over the condition of Jerusalem and his people was expressed in his reference to tombs and gates. A tomb was a place to show respect for dead community members who birthed the living generation and passed on their spiritual values to them. Tombs were also the place where the present generation hoped to be honored by burial at death. Gates were emblematic of the life of the city, since the people gathered for judicial procedure or basic social interaction near the gates. The burned gates represented the death of social life, that is, the end of a community of people.

What do you request? (v. 4)—The king rightly interpreted Nehemiah's sad countenance as a desire to take action on behalf of his people and homeland. His immediate response to the king's question illustrates how continual his prayer life was (see 1:6).

that I may rebuild it (v. 5)—The request undeniably referred to the city walls, for there could be

me; I told no one what my God had put in my heart to do at Jerusalem; nor was there any animal with me, except the one on which I rode.

13 And I went out by night through the Valley Gate to the Serpent Well and the Refuse Gate, and viewed the walls of Jerusalem which were broken down and its gates which were burned with fire.

14 Then I went on to the Fountain Gate and to the King's Pool, but there was no room for the animal under me to pass.

15 o I went up in the night by the valley, and viewed the wall; then I turned back and entered by the Valley Gate, and so returned.

16 And the officials did not know where I had gone or what I had done; I had not yet told the Jews, the priests, the nobles, the officials, or the others who did the work.

17 Then I said to them, "You see the distress that we are in, how Jerusalem lies waste, and its gates are burned with fire. Come and let us build the wall of Jerusalem, that we may no longer be a reproach."

18 And I told them of the hand of my God which had been good upon me, and also of the king's words that he had spoken to me. So they said, "Let us rise up and build." Then they set their hands to this good work.

19 But when Sanballat the Horonite, Tobiah the Ammonite official, and Geshem the Arab heard of it, they laughed at us and despised us, and said, "What is this thing that you are doing? Will you rebel against the king?"

20 So I answered them, and said to them, "The God of heaven Himself will prosper us; therefore we His servants will arise and build, but you have no heritage or right or memorial in Jerusalem."

no permanence without walls, but it also may have included political and administrative rebuilding as well.

the queen (v. 6)—Since Esther was the queen of the previous king Ahasuerus (Xerxes) about 486–464 B.C. and possibly the stepmother of Artaxerxes, it could be that she had previously influenced the present king and queen to be favorably disposed to the Jews.

return (v. 6)—This presupposes that Nehemiah was being dispatched on his desired mission and upon its completion would return to Persia.

let letters be given to me (v. 7)—Official letters transferred a portion of the king's authority to Nehemiah. In this context, he needed to pass through the lands of Judah's enemies, who could harm him or prevent him from rebuilding Jerusalem. The roads upon which messengers, ambassadors, and envoys of all sorts traveled had stations where such letters could be inspected for passage. Three months of travel from Susa to Jerusalem was long, dangerous, and ridden with protocol where letters were required for passage. The danger associated with the passage, but particularly the administrative authority which Nehemiah carried in the letters, led Artaxerxes to send captains of the army and horsemen with Nehemiah for protection (2:9).

and a letter to Asaph the keeper of the king's forest (v. 8)—Lumber was a very precious commodity. This is illustrated in a document from one ancient city in Mesopotamia in which a forest official is taken to court for cutting down a tree. Forests were carefully guarded, and written permission from the king would assure Nehemiah of the lumber he would need to build the citadel, wall reinforcements, and his own residence from which he would administrate the reconstruction.

citadel (v. 8)—This edifice located next to the temple on the northwest side was a fortified building for the purpose of guarding the temple. It was subsequently rebuilt by Herod and named Antonia.

the good hand of my God upon me (v. 8)—This refrain is common to both Ezra and Nehemiah. It is a frequent reminder in these inspired books that God works through His servants to accomplish His will.

I went to the governors (v. 9)—Nehemiah's encroachment upon their provincial control posed a tremendous threat to these officials. If handled improperly, disregard for the other local officials would have put Nehemiah's life and the lives of those in Jerusalem in jeopardy. To prevent such a reaction, God had moved the Persian king to dispatch royal army captains and horsemen to accompany Nehemiah and to guard against such attacks.

Sanballat . . . Tobiah (v. 10)—These men were probably also behind the opposition described in Ezra 4:7–23 which stopped the work in Jerusalem. Sanballat served as governor of Samaria (Horonaim being a town in Moab, he was probably a Moabite) and Tobiah of the region east of the Jordan. These district magistrates were leaders of Samaritan factions (see chapter 6) to the north and east. They had lost any recourse to prevent Judah from rebuilding since God's people were authorized to fortify their settlement against attack from enemies such as these two officials. To overtly attack or oppose the Jews would be to oppose the Persian king.

was there three days (v. 11)—Nehemiah spent three days discerning what course to follow before informing anyone of his plan; then, he wisely viewed the terrain in secret and surveyed the southern end of the city, noting the broken and burnt conditions of the walls and gates.

Valley Gate (vv. 13, 15)—Nehemiah began and ended his trip at the same spot (see 3:13) on the west side.

Serpent Well (v. 13)—The exact location is unknown, although it is somewhere in the southern section of Jerusalem.

Refuse Gate (v. 13)—a.k.a. Dung Gate; at the southern tip of the city (see 3:13; 12:31) a common sewer ran to the Kidron Brook into the Valley of Hinnom

Fountain Gate (v. 14)—The exact location is unknown, although it was somewhere in the southern section of Jerusalem, probably on the east side.

King's Pool (v. 14)—possibly the pool of Siloam (see 3:15)

the valley (v. 15)—the Kidron Valley, running north and south to the east of the temple mount

we may no longer be a reproach (v. 17)—The destruction of the city by Nebuchadnezzar brought great reproach upon Israel, but particularly upon their God. Nehemiah assured the Jews (v. 20) that because God would prosper them in this endeavor for His glory, they should move ahead.

"Let us rise up" (v. 18)—The sight of Nehemiah's credentials and his motivating message revived their drooping spirits to begin the building despite the bitter taunts of influential men (vv. 19–20).

Geshem the Arab (v. 19)—This ruler most likely officiated to the south of Jerusalem.

God of heaven (v. 20)—Not only did Nehemiah have the king's permission and was not rebelling, but he had God's protection. Those enemies who tried to intimidate against the work had neither, since they were not commissioned by God or the king.

Understanding the Text

5) What events transpired to present Nehemiah the opportunity to speak to the king about his concern?

_____

_____

_____

_____

6) What was Nehemiah's frame of mind at the beginning of chapter 2, and why did the king's question make him afraid? What wise thing did Nehemiah do when afraid?

_____

_____

_____

_____

(verses to consider: Psalm 56:3; Isaiah 41:10)

7) What did Nehemiah request of the king?

_____

_____

_____

_____

8) What did Nehemiah do during his first three days in Jerusalem?

_____

_____

_____

_____

(verses to consider: Psalm 62:1–7; Isaiah 30:15)

9) What "homework" or secret project did Nehemiah undertake before challenging the people to rebuild the walls?

_____

_____

_____

_____

(verses to consider: Proverbs 15:22; 16:3, 9; 19:21; 21:5)

Cross Reference

Read Acts 5:27–39.

²⁷ *And when they had brought them, they set them before the council. And the high priest asked them,*

²⁸ *saying, "Did we not strictly command you not to teach in this name? And look, you have filled Jerusalem with your doctrine, and intend to bring this Man's blood on us!"*

²⁹ *But Peter and the other apostles answered and said: "We ought to obey God rather than men.*

³⁰ *"The God of our fathers raised up Jesus whom you murdered by hanging on a tree.*

³¹ *"Him God has exalted to His right hand to be Prince and Savior, to give repentance to Israel and forgiveness of sins.*

³² *"And we are His witnesses to these things, and so also is the Holy Spirit whom God has given to those who obey Him."*

³³ *When they heard this, they were furious and plotted to kill them.*

³⁴ *Then one in the council stood up, a Pharisee named Gamaliel, a teacher of the law held in respect by all the people, and commanded them to put the apostles outside for a little while.*

³⁵ *And he said to them: "Men of Israel, take heed to yourselves what you intend to do regarding these men.*

³⁶ *"For some time ago Theudas rose up, claiming to be somebody. A number of men, about four hundred, joined him. He was slain, and all who obeyed him were scattered and came to nothing.*

37 *"After this man, Judas of Galilee rose up in the days of the census, and drew away many people after him. He also perished, and all who obeyed him were dispersed.*

38 *"And now I say to you, keep away from these men and let them alone; for if this plan or this work is of men, it will come to nothing;*

39 *"but if it is of God, you cannot overthrow it—lest you even be found to fight against God."*

Exploring the Meaning

10) In what ways was the Sanhedrin's opposition to the apostles similar to the way Sanballat, Tobiah, and Geshem opposed Nehemiah?

_____

_____

_____

_____

11) Consider that Nehemiah waited and prayed for perhaps four months before taking action regarding the walls of Jerusalem. Then read Psalm 5:3. Why is waiting so hard for most of us? Why is it so important?

_____

_____

_____

_____

(verses to consider: Psalm 27:14; 33:20; 37:7, 34; 130:5; Isaiah 26:8)

12) Read Genesis 39:2–4. Who is ultimately behind any and all of our successes?

_____

_____

_____

(verses to consider: Genesis 39:20–23; 2 Samuel 8:14; Ezra 1:5; 7:6)

13) Why was Nehemiah so confident that the Lord would grant them success?

_____

_____

_____

_____

Summing Up...

"Making sensible and careful plans for serving God does not conflict with reliance on His providence, and reliance on His providence does not excuse failure to plan."—*John MacArthur*

Reflecting on the Text

14) What problem or situation in your life do you want to confront with greater boldness this week? How can Nehemiah's life serve as a pattern for you?

_____

_____

_____

_____

15) What were the concrete ways Nehemiah demonstrated dependence on God? What are some specific ways you can better trust God this week?

_____

_____

_____

_____

16) What were the concrete ways Nehemiah planned and prepared for his wall-building endeavor? What are some specific ways you can better plan and prepare in your service of God this week?

_____

_____

_____

_____

17) How can you respond to criticism in a more God-honoring fashion in the future?

_____

_____

_____

_____

Recording Your Thoughts

_____

_____

_____

_____

_____

_____

For further study, see the following passages:

Ezra 1:2	Ezra 1:11	Ezra 7:8–9
Nehemiah 5:1–3	Nehemiah 13:6	Esther 4:11
Isaiah 51:7		

Wall Builders!

Nehemiah 3:1–32

Opening Thought

1) What is the most involved and extensive construction or remodeling project you've ever attempted? What did you learn from this experience?

_____

_____

_____

_____

2) When have you enjoyed positive experiences of working with others to accomplish a task? What is your all-time worst experience of "teamwork"? What happened?

_____

_____

_____

_____

3) What are the best lessons you've learned about how to get a group of diverse people to come together to complete a singular task?

_____

_____

_____

_____

Background of the Passage

Nehemiah was a man with a great burden to do a significant work for God and for His people (see 2:12). Specifically, this trusted Jewish adviser to the Persian king Artaxerxes had been overcome by sadness upon learning that the walls and gates of Jerusalem were in shambles (1:4). His shock eventually turned into conviction (1:6, 7), and this eventually led to a passionate desire to change the status quo. When God finally revealed through sovereign circumstances that the time was right to act (see 2:1–4), Nehemiah courageously stepped forward in faith and was granted permission by the Persian king to return to the land of his forefathers to lead an effort to rebuild the walls of Jerusalem.

Following a long and dangerous journey (see 2:11), coupled with much prayer and careful preparation (see 1:5–11; 2:4, 7, 8, 11–16), Nehemiah gathered the citizens of Jerusalem and challenged them to come together to rebuild the city's walls. He motivated them, not only with a vision of a secure future (2:17), but also with a reminder of God's past faithfulness (2:18). Their response was favorable. The project began in earnest.

At first glance chapter 3 of Nehemiah seems to be nothing more than a simple list of the workers who participated in the rebuilding effort. But further inspection reveals a numbering of fascinating insights about leadership, human nature, and hard work.

Bible Passage

Read 3:1–32, noting the key words and definitions to the right of the passage.

Nehemiah 3:1–32:

¹ *Then Eliashib the high priest rose up with his brethren the priests and built the Sheep Gate; they consecrated it and hung its doors. They built as far as the Tower of the Hundred, and consecrated it, then as far as the Tower of Hananel.*

² *Next to Eliashib the men of Jericho built. And next to them Zaccur the son of Imri built.*

³ *Also the sons of Hassenaah built the Fish Gate; they laid its beams and hung its doors with its bolts and bars.*

Eliashib the high priest (v. 1) —the grandson of Jeshua the high priest in Zerubbabel's era (see Neh. 12:10)

built (v. 1)—on the fourth of Ab (Jul./Aug.), 445 B.C. (see 6:15)

Sheep Gate (v. 1)—This is located in the northeast section of Jerusalem (see 3:32; 12:39). The narrative moves around the perimeter of Jerusalem in a counterclockwise direction.

4 *And next to them Meremoth the son of Urijah, the son of Koz, made repairs. Next to them Meshullam the son of Berechiah, the son of Meshezabel, made repairs. Next to them Zadok the son of Baana made repairs.*

5 *Next to them the Tekoites made repairs; but their nobles did not put their shoulders to the work of their Lord.*

6 *Moreover Jehoiada the son of Paseah and Meshullam the son of Besodeiah repaired the Old Gate; they laid its beams and hung its doors, with its bolts and bars.*

7 *And next to them Melatiah the Gibeonite, Jadon the Meronothite, the men of Gibeon and Mizpah, repaired the residence of the governor of the region beyond the River.*

8 *Next to him Uzziel the son of Harhaiah, one of the goldsmiths, made repairs. Also next to him Hananiah, one of the perfumers, made repairs; and they fortified Jerusalem as far as the Broad Wall.*

9 *And next to them Rephaiah the son of Hur, leader of half the district of Jerusalem, made repairs.*

10 *Next to them Jedaiah the son of Harumaph made repairs in front of his house. And next to him Hattush the son of Hashabniah made repairs.*

11 *Malchijah the son of Harim and Hashub the son of Pahath-Moab repaired another section, as well as the Tower of the Ovens.*

12 *And next to him was Shallum the son of Hallohesh, leader of half the district of Jerusalem; he and his daughters made repairs.*

13 *Hanun and the inhabitants of Zanoah repaired the Valley Gate. They built it, hung its doors with its bolts and bars, and repaired a thousand cubits of the wall as far as the Refuse Gate.*

14 *Malchijah the son of Rechab, leader of the district of Beth Haccerem, repaired the Refuse Gate; he built it and hung its doors with its bolts and bars.*

15 *Shallun the son of Col-Hozeh, leader of the district of Mizpah, repaired the Fountain Gate; he built it, covered it, hung its doors with its bolts*

Tower of the Hundred . . . Tower of Hananel (v. 1)—This northern section of Jerusalem opened up to the central Benjamin plateau where enemy forces could attack most easily from the north. The rest of the perimeter of the city was protected by the natural valley topography.

Fish Gate (v. 3)—This was so named because merchants sold fish on the northern side of Jerusalem. Men of Tyre and other seacoast towns routinely brought fish to sell (see 12:39; 13:16).

nobles did not put their shoulders to the work of their Lord (v. 5)—One explanation, beyond just the laziness of the rich, is that these nobles had given their loyalty to Tobiah for personal gain (6:17–19).

the Old Gate (v. 6)—believed to be in the northwest corner of Jerusalem (see 12:39)

the Broad Wall (v. 8)—on the western side of the northern sector (see 12:38)

Tower of the Ovens (v. 11)—on the western side of Jerusalem (see 12:38)

the Valley Gate (v. 13)—see 2:13, 15

the Refuse Gate (v. 13)—see 2:13

Pool of Shelah (v. 15)—see 2:14

the King's Garden (v. 15)—in the southeast sector

and bars, and repaired the wall of the Pool of Shelah by the King's Garden, as far as the stairs that go down from the City of David.

16 After him Nehemiah the son of Azbuk, leader of half the district of Beth Zur, made repairs as far as the place in front of the tombs of David, to the man-made pool, and as far as the House of the Mighty.

17 After him the Levites, under Rehum the son of Bani, made repairs. Next to him Hashabiah, leader of half the district of Keilah, made repairs for his district.

18 After him their brethren, under Bavai the son of Henadad, leader of the other half of the district of Keilah, made repairs.

19 And next to him Ezer the son of Jeshua, the leader of Mizpah, repaired another section in front of the Ascent to the Armory at the buttress.

20 After him Baruch the son of Zabbai carefully repaired the other section, from the buttress to the door of the house of Eliashib the high priest.

21 After him Meremoth the son of Urijah, the son of Koz, repaired another section, from the door of the house of Eliashib to the end of the house of Eliashib.

22 And after him the priests, the men of the plain, made repairs.

23 After him Benjamin and Hasshub made repairs opposite their house. After them Azariah the son of Maaseiah, the son of Ananiah, made repairs by his house.

24 After him Binnui the son of Henadad repaired another section, from the house of Azariah to the buttress, even as far as the corner.

25 Palal the son of Uzai made repairs opposite the buttress, and on the tower which projects from the king's upper house that was by the court of the prison. After him Pedaiah the son of Parosh made repairs.

26 Moreover the Nethinim who dwelt in Ophel made repairs as far as the place in front of the Water Gate toward the east, and on the projecting tower.

27 After them the Tekoites repaired another section,

tombs of David (v. 16)—see 2:5; presumably in the southeast sector

House of the Mighty (v. 16)—This location is probably associated with David's mighty men (see 2 Sam. 23:8–39).

the Armory (v. 19)—located on the eastern side of Jerusalem

Ophel (v. 26)—an area south of the temple mount, near the Water Gate, where the Nethinim lived (see 2 Chr. 27:3; 33:14; Neh. 11:21)

the Water Gate (v. 26)—near the Gihon Spring on the east side of Jerusalem (see 8:16; 12:37) *next to the great projecting tower, and as far as the wall of Ophel.*

28 *Beyond the Horse Gate the priests made repairs, each in front of his own house.*

29 *After them Zadok the son of Immer made repairs in front of his own house. After him Shemaiah the son of Shechaniah, the keeper of the East Gate, made repairs.*

30 *After him Hananiah the son of Shelemiah, and Hanun, the sixth son of Zalaph, repaired another section. After him Meshullam the son of Berechiah made repairs in front of his dwelling.*

31 *After him Malchijah, one of the goldsmiths, made repairs as far as the house of the Nethinim and of the merchants, in front of the Miphkad Gate, and as far as the upper room at the corner.*

32 *And between the upper room at the corner, as far as the Sheep Gate, the goldsmiths and the merchants made repairs.*

the Horse Gate (v. 28)—in the northeast sector

the East Gate (v. 29)—possibly located to the east of the temple mount

the Miphkad Gate (v. 31)—in the northeast sector

the Sheep Gate (v. 32)—Having traveled around Jerusalem in a counterclockwise direction, the narrative ends where it began (see 3:1; 12:39).

Understanding the Text

4) How did the religious leaders set an example for the rest of the populace (v. 1)?

_____

_____

_____

_____

5) What kinds of people were involved in this rebuilding effort? (List the various occupations mentioned in the chapter.)

_____

_____

_____

_____

6) Why did Nehemiah and the people concentrate so intensely on the repair of Jerusalem's gates?

_____

_____

_____

_____

7) What does the chapter say about the noblemen of Tekoa?

_____

_____

_____

_____

8) What criteria did Nehemiah use in deciding who would work where (see vv. 10, 28, 30)?

_____

_____

_____

_____

Cross Reference

Read 1 Corinthians 12.

¹ *Now concerning spiritual gifts, brethren, I do not want you to be ignorant:*
² *You know that you were Gentiles, carried away to these dumb idols, however you were led.*
³ *Therefore I make known to you that no one speaking by the Spirit of God calls Jesus accursed, and no one can say that Jesus is Lord except by the Holy Spirit.*
⁴ *There are diversities of gifts, but the same Spirit.*
⁵ *There are differences of ministries, but the same Lord.*
⁶ *And there are diversities of activities, but it is the same God who works all in all.*

⁷ But the manifestation of the Spirit is given to each one for the profit of all:

⁸ for to one is given the word of wisdom through the Spirit, to another the word of knowledge through the same Spirit,

⁹ to another faith by the same Spirit, to another gifts of healings by the same Spirit,

¹⁰ to another the working of miracles, to another prophecy, to another discerning of spirits, to another different kinds of tongues, to another the interpretation of tongues.

¹¹ But one and the same Spirit works all these things, distributing to each one individually as He wills.

¹² For as the body is one and has many members, but all the members of that one body, being many, are one body, so also is Christ.

¹³ For by one Spirit we were all baptized into one body-whether Jews or Greeks, whether slaves or free-and have all been made to drink into one Spirit.

¹⁴ For in fact the body is not one member but many.

¹⁵ If the foot should say, "Because I am not a hand, I am not of the body," is it therefore not of the body?

¹⁶ And if the ear should say, "Because I am not an eye, I am not of the body," is it therefore not of the body?

¹⁷ If the whole body were an eye, where would be the hearing? If the whole were hearing, where would be the smelling?

¹⁸ But now God has set the members, each one of them, in the body just as He pleased.

¹⁹ And if they were all one member, where would the body be?

²⁰ But now indeed there are many members, yet one body.

²¹ And the eye cannot say to the hand, "I have no need of you"; nor again the head to the feet, "I have no need of you."

²² No, much rather, those members of the body which seem to be weaker are necessary.

²³ And those members of the body which we think to be less honorable, on these we bestow greater honor; and our unpresentable parts have greater modesty,

²⁴ but our presentable parts have no need. But God composed the body, having given greater honor to that part which lacks it,

²⁵ that there should be no schism in the body, but that the members should have the same care for one another.

²⁶ And if one member suffers, all the members suffer with it; or if one member is honored, all the members rejoice with it.

²⁷ Now you are the body of Christ, and members individually.

²⁸ And God has appointed these in the church: first apostles, second prophets, third teachers, after that miracles, then gifts of healings, helps, administrations, varieties of tongues.

²⁹ *Are all apostles? Are all prophets? Are all teachers? Are all workers of miracles?*
³⁰ *Do all have gifts of healings? Do all speak with tongues? Do all interpret?*
³¹ *But earnestly desire the best gifts. And yet I show you a more excellent way.*

Exploring the Meaning

9) How do Paul's words to the church at Corinth shed light on the events of Nehemiah 3?

_____

_____

_____

_____

10) Read 1 Kings 5:1–18. What similarities do you see between Solomon's building project (the temple) and Nehemiah's (Jerusalem's walls)? What differences?

_____

_____

_____

_____

11) Read Romans 12:10–11. What does it mean to be "fervent" or "zealous" in serving God (see Neh. 3:20)? Why is attitude important?

_____

_____

_____

_____

12) Read Proverbs 14:23. What does this verse say about the importance of working hard?

_____

Summing Up...

"Essential to unity is diversity. Unity of spirit and purpose can be maintained only through diversity of ministry. But unity is not uniformity. A football team whose players all wanted to play quarterback would have uniformity but not unity. It could not function as a team if everyone played the same position."—*John MacArthur*

Reflecting on the Text

13) Warren Wiersbe has written: "British humorist Jerome K. Jerome said, 'I like work, it fascinates me. I can sit and look at it for hours.' When it comes to the work of the Lord, there is no place for spectators or self-appointed advisors and critics; but there is always room for workers." Be Determined, Colorado Springs: Chariot Victor, 1992, p. 37

How would you assess your own participation in the ministries of your church? Are you a tireless laborer or a slacker? If someone wrote a summary (similar to Neh. 3) regarding who is doing what in your church, would you be listed favorably or unfavorably? Why?

_____

_____

_____

_____

14) What does this chapter teach you about accomplishing an overwhelming task? What overwhelming "construction project" are you facing in your own life? in your church?

_____

_____

15) What steps can you take this week to depend on God and others even as you do your part in confronting the challenges in your life?

_____

_____

_____

_____

_____

Recording Your Thoughts

_____

_____

_____

_____

_____

_____

_____

_____

_____

_____

For further study, see the following passages:

2 Chronicles 23:15	Ecclesiastes 9:10	John 17:4
1 Corinthians 10:31	1 Corinthians 14	1 Corinthians 15:58
Ephesians 2:10	Ephesians 6:5–8	Philippians 1:13
1 Timothy 5:4	Revelation 2:2	

Opposition to the Work

Opening Thought

1) What do you consider some of the most blatant modern-day examples of opposition to God, His plan, or His people?

_____

_____

2) What kind of criticism or opposition is most difficult for you to take:
- at the hands of strangers (perhaps unbelievers)?
- at the hands of fellow church members?
- at the hands of family members?
- Other: _____ (specify)?

Why is that most difficult?

_____

_____

3) What is jealousy? What is behind this powerful emotion that prompts people to become agitated and upset when others succeed?

_____

_____

4) When in your life have you felt the strongest opposition to accomplishing something you felt God was leading you to do?

_____

_____

Background of the Passage

Here is a statement you can write down and bank on:

When God's people attempt to do God's work in God's way, there will always be opposition.

It's true. The Bible records this fact. History confirms it repeatedly. The enemies of God will do everything in their power to thwart His purposes. They will never sit idly by and allow God to receive glory or permit His people to experience victory-not, at least, without a severe fight.

Following the remarkable series of successes recorded in Nehemiah 1–3 (Nehemiah having his prayers answered, getting royal permission to return to Jerusalem, being granted government resources, authority, and protection, receiving an enthusiastic response from his countrymen, etc.), Nehemiah 4 details a severe crisis in the attempt to rebuild the walls of Jerusalem.

Sanballat, Tobiah, and Geshem (see 2:10, 19) incited their followers to oppose the reconstruction effort. As these human enemies ridiculed God's people and plotted against them, other, more sinister, spiritual forces attempted to stop the work by filling the Israelites with discouragement and fear.

Nehemiah demonstrated remarkable leadership skills in keeping his work force focused and faithful. This chapter is a wonderful case study in how to persevere in the face of intense antagonism. It also reveals how opposition, rightly handled, can actually become a tool in the hands of God to make His people stronger in their quest to do His will.

Bible Passage

Read 4:1–23, noting the key words and definitions to the right of the passage.

Nehemiah 4:1–23:

¹ *But it so happened, when Sanballat heard that we were rebuilding the wall, that he was furious and very indignant, and mocked the Jews.*
² *And he spoke before his brethren and the army of*

the army of Samaria (v. 2)—
While it is a possibility that his intentions were to provoke the military force to action, since that would have brought the Persian overlord down on Samaria swiftly, harassment and mockery (v. 3)

Samaria, and said, "What are these feeble Jews doing? Will they fortify themselves? Will they offer sacrifices? Will they complete it in a day? Will they revive the stones from the heaps of rubbish-stones that are burned?"

3 Now Tobiah the Ammonite was beside him, and he said, "Whatever they build, if even a fox goes up on it, he will break down their stone wall."

4 Hear, O our God, for we are despised; turn their reproach on their own heads, and give them as plunder to a land of captivity!

5 Do not cover their iniquity, and do not let their sin be blotted out from before You; for they have provoked You to anger before the builders.

6 So we built the wall, and the entire wall was joined together up to half its height, for the people had a mind to work.

7 Now it happened, when Sanballat, Tobiah, the Arabs, the Ammonites, and the Ashdodites heard that the walls of Jerusalem were being restored and the gaps were beginning to be closed, that they became very angry,

8 and all of them conspired together to come and attack Jerusalem and create confusion.

9 Nevertheless we made our prayer to our God, and because of them we set a watch against them day and night.

10 Then Judah said, "The strength of the laborers is failing, and there is so much rubbish that we are not able to build the wall."

11 And our adversaries said, "They will neither know nor see anything, till we come into their midst and kill them and cause the work to cease."

12 So it was, when the Jews who dwelt near them came, that they told us ten times, "From whatever place you turn, they will be upon us."

13 Therefore I positioned men behind the lower parts of the wall, at the openings; and I set the people

became the primary strategy to prevent the reconstruction of the walls.

Hear, O our God (vv. 4–5)—Nehemiah's dependence on his sovereign God is never more evident than in his prayer (see 1:5–11; 2:4).

the Ashdodites (vv. 7–8)—Added to the list of enemies already given are the dwellers of Ashdod, one of the former Philistine cities to the west of Jerusalem. Apparently they came to the point where they were at least contemplating a full-scale attack on Jerusalem because of the rapid progress of the wall.

we made our prayer . . . we set a watch (v. 9)—The Jews exhibited a balance between faith in God and readiness, employing some of the wall builders as guards.

so much rubbish (v. 10)—Literally "dust," the term refers to the rubble or ruins of the prior destruction (586 B.C.), which they had to clear away before they could make significant progress on the rebuilding of the walls.

And our adversaries said (v. 11)—Part of the strategy of the enemy coalition was to frighten and intimidate the Jews by making them think their army would soon surprise them with a massive force that would quickly engulf them.

positioned men (vv. 13–15)—Nehemiah and the others had received word that Sanballat had mustered the army of Samaria (4:2). In fact, God made sure the strategy was known by letting the nearby Jews know, so they would report it to Judah's leaders. Though vigilant, armed, and ready, Nehemiah and those he led con-

according to their families, with their swords, their spears, and their bows.

14 *And I looked, and arose and said to the nobles, to the leaders, and to the rest of the people, "Do not be afraid of them. Remember the Lord, great and awesome, and fight for your brethren, your sons, your daughters, your wives, and your houses."*

15 *And it happened, when our enemies heard that it was known to us, and that God had brought their plot to nothing, that all of us returned to the wall, everyone to his work.*

16 *So it was, from that time on, that half of my servants worked at construction, while the other half held the spears, the shields, the bows, and wore armor; and the leaders were behind all the house of Judah.*

17 *Those who built on the wall, and those who carried burdens, loaded themselves so that with one hand they worked at construction, and with the other held a weapon.*

18 *Every one of the builders had his sword girded at his side as he built. And the one who sounded the trumpet was beside me.*

19 *Then I said to the nobles, the rulers, and the rest of the people, "The work is great and extensive, and we are separated far from one another on the wall.*

20 *"Wherever you hear the sound of the trumpet, rally to us there. Our God will fight for us."*

21 *So we labored in the work, and half of the men held the spears from daybreak until the stars appeared.*

22 *At the same time I also said to the people, "Let each man and his servant stay at night in Jerusalem, that they may be our guard by night and a working party by day."*

23 *So neither I, my brethren, my servants, nor the men of the guard who followed me took off our clothes, except that everyone took them off for washing.*

sistently gave God the glory for their victories and construction successes.

half of my servants worked (vv. 16–18a)—The threats cut the work force in half, and even those who worked carried weapons in case of attack (see v. 21).

trumpet (v. 18b–20)—Among other functions, trumpets were used to sound an alarm in the event of danger or to summon soldiers to battle. Nehemiah kept a trumpeter at his side always, so that the alarm could be sounded immediately. His plan also included perpetual diligence (vv. 22–23).

Understanding the Text

5) What tactics did Sanballat and Tobiah use to discourage the Jews from rebuilding the city walls?

_____

_____

_____

_____

_____

_____

6) How did Nehemiah respond specifically to the taunts and plots of his enemies (4:4–5)?

_____

_____

_____

_____

_____

7) According to Nehemiah (4:6), why were the Jews so successful in their work?

_____

_____

_____

_____

_____

_____

8) Did the Jews rely on divine protection or human planning/effort in attempting to protect themselves from their enemies? What makes you say this? Which of the two strategies is more important? Why?

_____

_____

_____

_____

_____

(verse to look at: Eph. 6:18; Col. 4:2–4)

Cross Reference

Read 2 Chronicles 32:1–23.

1 *After these deeds of faithfulness, Sennacherib king of Assyria came and entered Judah; he encamped against the fortified cities, thinking to win them over to himself.*

2 *And when Hezekiah saw that Sennacherib had come, and that his purpose was to make war against Jerusalem,*

3 *he consulted with his leaders and commanders to stop the water from the springs which were outside the city; and they helped him.*

4 *Thus many people gathered together who stopped all the springs and the brook that ran through the land, saying, "Why should the kings of Assyria come and find much water?"*

5 *And he strengthened himself, built up all the wall that was broken, raised it up to the towers, and built another wall outside; also he repaired the Millo in the City of David, and made weapons and shields in abundance.*

6 *Then he set military captains over the people, gathered them together to him in the open square of the city gate, and gave them encouragement, saying,*

7 *"Be strong and courageous; do not be afraid nor dismayed before the king of Assyria, nor before all the multitude that is with him; for there are more with us than with him.*

8 *With him is an arm of flesh; but with us is the LORD our God, to help us and to fight our battles." And the people were strengthened by the words of Hezekiah king of Judah.*

⁹ *After this Sennacherib king of Assyria sent his servants to Jerusalem (but he and all the forces with him laid siege against Lachish), to Hezekiah king of Judah, and to all Judah who were in Jerusalem, saying,*

¹⁰ *"Thus says Sennacherib king of Assyria: 'In what do you trust, that you remain under siege in Jerusalem?*

¹¹ *"'Does not Hezekiah persuade you to give yourselves over to die by famine and by thirst, saying, "The LORD our God will deliver us from the hand of the king of Assyria"?*

¹² *"'Has not the same Hezekiah taken away His high places and His altars, and commanded Judah and Jerusalem, saying, "You shall worship before one altar and burn incense on it"?*

¹³ *"'Do you not know what I and my fathers have done to all the peoples of other lands? Were the gods of the nations of those lands in any way able to deliver their lands out of my hand?*

¹⁴ *"'Who was there among all the gods of those nations that my fathers utterly destroyed that could deliver his people from my hand, that your God should be able to deliver you from my hand?*

¹⁵ *"'Now therefore, do not let Hezekiah deceive you or persuade you like this, and do not believe him; for no god of any nation or kingdom was able to deliver his people from my hand or the hand of my fathers. How much less will your God deliver you from my hand?'"*

¹⁶ *Furthermore, his servants spoke against the LORD God and against His servant Hezekiah.*

¹⁷ *He also wrote letters to revile the LORD God of Israel, and to speak against Him, saying, "As the gods of the nations of other lands have not delivered their people from my hand, so the God of Hezekiah will not deliver His people from my hand."*

¹⁸ *Then they called out with a loud voice in Hebrew to the people of Jerusalem who were on the wall, to frighten them and trouble them, that they might take the city.*

¹⁹ *And they spoke against the God of Jerusalem, as against the gods of the people of the earth-the work of men's hands.*

²⁰ *Now because of this King Hezekiah and the prophet Isaiah, the son of Amoz, prayed and cried out to heaven.*

²¹ *Then the LORD sent an angel who cut down every mighty man of valor, leader, and captain in the camp of the king of Assyria. So he returned shamefaced to his own land. And when he had gone into the temple of his god, some of his own offspring struck him down with the sword there.*

²² *Thus the LORD saved Hezekiah and the inhabitants of Jerusalem from the hand*

of Sennacherib the king of Assyria, and from the hand of all others, and guided them on every side.

²³ *And many brought gifts to the LORD at Jerusalem, and presents to Hezekiah king of Judah, so that he was exalted in the sight of all nations thereafter.*

Exploring the Meaning

9) How was the situation Hezekiah faced similar to the events described in Nehemiah 4? What similarities do you see in the way these two leaders responded to extreme hostility and overt threats?

_____

_____

_____

_____

_____

_____

10) Read 1 Samuel 17:41–47. How did Goliath ridicule and threaten David? What was the outcome of this contest? Why?

_____

_____

_____

_____

_____

_____

11) Read 1 Corinthians 1:18–31. What does this passage say about God using feeble tools or persons to accomplish His work?

_____

_____

_____

_____

_____

_____

Summing Up...

"Perseverance in the Christian life is a ceaseless warfare against the forces of the kingdom of darkness (see Eph. 6:10–19.). Christians therefore need to be reminded to expect hardships and persecution and not be dismayed by them. Jesus promised that 'in the world you have tribulation' (John 16:33). 'Suffer hardship with me, as a good soldier of Christ Jesus,' Paul exhorted Timothy, since 'all who desire to live godly in Christ Jesus will be persecuted' (2 Tim. 2:3; 3:12). James gave the good news that such tribulation produces spiritual endurance (James 1:2–4)."—*John MacArthur*

Reflecting on the Text

12) What do you most appreciate about Nehemiah and the Israelites in this chapter? Why? What lessons or principles do you see for your own life?

_____

_____

_____

_____

_____

13) In future instances of opposition, how do you plan to respond in a fashion that pleases and honors God?

_____

_____

_____

_____

_____

_____

14) To what project or church endeavor do you need to renew your commitment (regardless of the opposition you might face)?

_____

_____

_____

_____

_____

Recording Your Thoughts

_____

_____

_____

_____

_____

_____

_____

For further study, see the following passages:

Numbers 32:9	Deuteronomy 20:8	Psalm 2:4
Psalm 139:19–22	Matthew 8:26	Matthew 13:25
Mark 13:33	Luke 22:63–65	Luke 23:12
1 Corinthians 15:58	2 Corinthians 10:1–6	James 1:5–8

Walls Between the Wall Builders!

Nehemiah 5:1–19

Opening Thought

1) How can socio-economic differences cause problems in a church or between believers?

_____

_____

_____

2) Why do you think so many Christians today are in such deep debt? What are the effects of financial strain on a person/family/church?

_____

_____

_____

3) How do you feel when your church leaders exhort you to give? Or when parachurch organizations send requests for financial support?

_____

_____

4) Many Christians use the excuse "I'd give more if I had more income." And yet, when raises come, oftentimes there is no substantial increase in the amount given. Why?

_____

_____

Background of the Passage

The first four chapters of Nehemiah remind us that any significant work for God can expect opposition. The devil will not sit idly by and watch God's people do great works to the glory of God. But attacks do not only come from without. Sometimes the enemy also seeks to work mischief from within.

This was the situation in Nehemiah 5. Enemy opposition and difficult times in general had precipitated dire economic conditions. Specifically, the people were fatigued with hard labor, drained by the relentless harassment of enemies, poor and lacking the necessities of life, lacking tax money and borrowing for it, and working on the wall in the city rather than getting food from the country.

On top of these hardships came the complaint that certain wealthy Jews were exploiting their unfortunate countrymen. Rather than show compassion, these opportunists forced people to sell their homes and children, while giving them no opportunity to redeem them back. Under normal conditions, the Mosiac law offered the hope of releasing these young people through the remission of debts every seven years or in the fiftieth year of Jubilee (Lev. 25). This custom of redemption made it possible to "buy back" the enslaved individual at almost any time, but the desperate financial situation of Nehemiah's times made that appear impossible.

The effect of this extortion on the morale of the returnees was worse than the enemy opposition. Nehemiah 5 demonstrates the dangers of greed and selfishness. It also shows how godly leaders guide their people through explosive situations and potentially divisive times.

Bible Passage

Read 5:1–19, noting the key words and definitions to the right of the passage.

Nehemiah 5:1–19:

¹ *And there was a great outcry of the people and their wives against their Jewish brethren.*

² *For there were those who said, "We, our sons,*

Jewish brethren (vv. 1-5)—
Perhaps this refers again to the nobles who would not work and had alliances with the enemies (see 3:5).

and our daughters are many; therefore let us get grain, that we may eat and live."

3 There were also some who said, "We have mortgaged our lands and vineyards and houses, that we might buy grain because of the famine."

4 There were also those who said, "We have borrowed money for the king's tax on our lands and vineyards.

5 "Yet now our flesh is as the flesh of our brethren, our children as their children; and indeed we are forcing our sons and our daughters to be slaves, and some of our daughters have been brought into slavery. It is not in our power to redeem them, for other men have our lands and vineyards."

6 And I became very angry when I heard their outcry and these words.

7 After serious thought, I rebuked the nobles and rulers, and said to them, "Each of you is exacting usury from his brother." So I called a great assembly against them.

8 And I said to them, "According to our ability we have redeemed our Jewish brethren who were sold to the nations. Now indeed, will you even sell your brethren? Or should they be sold to us?" Then they were silenced and found nothing to say.

9 Then I said, "What you are doing is not good. Should you not walk in the fear of our God because of the reproach of the nations, our enemies?"

10 "I also, with my brethren and my servants, am lending them money and grain. Please, let us stop this usury!

11 "Restore now to them, even this day, their lands, their vineyards, their olive groves, and their houses, also a hundredth of the money and the grain, the new wine and the oil, that you have charged them."

12 So they said, "We will restore it, and will require

I rebuked the nobles and rulers (v. 7)—The commitment of the nobles and rulers to the reconstruction project was negligible (see 3:5), while their loyalty to Tobiah and others in opposition added to their opportunistic attitudes, placing them close to the status of opposition. They had become the enemy from within.

exacting usury (v. 7)—Usury can refer to normal interest or it can signify excessive interest. According to Mosaic law, the Jews were forbidden to take interest from their brothers on the loan of money, food, or anything else. If the person was destitute, they should consider it a gift. If the recipient could pay it back later, it was to be without interest. Such generosity marked the godly. Interest could be taken from foreigners. In the ancient world interest loans are known to have exceeded fifty percent at times. Such usury took advantage of people's desperation and was virtually impossible to repay, consuming their entire family assets and reducing the debtors to permanent slavery.

we have redeemed (v. 8)—Nehemiah denounced with just severity the evil conduct of selling a brother by means of usury. He contrasted it with his own action of redeeming with his own money some of the Jewish exiles, who through debt had lost their freedom in Babylon.

I also (v. 10)—Nehemiah set the example again by making loans, but not in exacting usury.

Restore now to them (v. 11)—To remedy the evil that they had brought, those guilty of usury were to return the property they had confiscated from those who couldn't pay the loans back, as well as returning the interest they had charged.

nothing from them; we will do as you say."
Then I called the priests, and required an oath
from them that they would do according to this
promise.

13 Then I shook out the fold of my garment and
said, "So may God shake out each man from his
house, and from his property, who does not perform this promise. Even thus may he be shaken
out and emptied." And all the assembly said,
"Amen!" and praised the LORD. Then the people
did according to this promise.

14 Moreover, from the time that I was appointed to
be their governor in the land of Judah, from the
twentieth year until the thirty-second year of King
Artaxerxes, twelve years, neither I nor my brothers ate the governor's provisions.

15 But the former governors who were before me laid
burdens on the people, and took from them bread
and wine, besides forty shekels of silver. Yes, even
their servants bore rule over the people, but I did
not do so, because of the fear of God.

16 Indeed, I also continued the work on this wall,
and we did not buy any land. All my servants
were gathered there for the work.

17 And at my table were one hundred and fifty Jews
and rulers, besides those who came to us from the
nations around us.

18 Now that which was prepared daily was one ox
and six choice sheep. Also fowl were prepared for
me, and once every ten days an abundance of all
kinds of wine. Yet in spite of this I did not
demand the governor's provisions, because the
bondage was heavy on this people.

19 Remember me, my God, for good, according to all
that I have done for this people.

an oath (v. 12)—The con-
sciences of the guilty were struck
by Nehemiah's words, so that their
fear, shame, and contrition caused
them to pledge the release of their
loans and restore property and
interest, including setting slaves
free. This cancellation of debt had
a profoundly unifying effect on
both sides of the indebtedness.
The proceedings were
formally consummated with the
people binding themselves with a
solemn oath administered by the
priests that they would be faithful
to the pledge.

shook out the fold (v. 13)—
This curse rite from the governor,
Nehemiah, called down God's
wrath upon anyone who would not
follow through with his commitment to release debts. The people
agreed and did as they had promised.

thirty-second year (v. 14)—the
year Nehemiah returned to
Artaxerxes in Persia (about 433
B.C.; see 13:6)

ate the governor's provisions
(v. 14)—This refers to the provisions from the Persian administration, but from which Nehemiah
had chosen not to partake
because it would have to come
from taxing his poverty-stricken
people (v. 15). The statement is
testimony to the wealth of
Nehemiah gained as the king's
cupbearer in Persia. Verses 17–18
record that he supported with
abundant provisions one hundred
fifty men who ruled with him (and
their families), indicating the personal wealth he had brought from
Babylon.

forty shekels (v. 15)—approxi-
mately one pound of silver

because of the fear of God
(v. 15)—Nehemiah would not
exact taxs from his fellow countrymen as his predecessors had,
because he viewed it as an act of
disobedience toward God.

we did not buy any land (v. 16)—Even though the time to purchase property from those forced to sell couldn't have been better, Nehemiah maintained a consistent personal policy not to take advantage of another's distress. He worked on the wall rather than spending his time building personal wealth.

governor's provisions (v. 18)—See 5:14. In the ancient Near East, it was customary to calculate the expense of a king's establishment, not by the quantity of money, but by the quantity of his provisions.

Remember me (v. 19)—the first of four such prayers (see 13:14, 22, 31)

Understanding the Text

5) What was the source of the conflict recorded in Nehemiah 5:1–5?

_____

_____

_____

6) What is "usury" (verse 7) and how was it a problem during the wall-building effort?

_____

_____

_____

(verses to consider: Leviticus 25:36, 37; Deuteronomy 23:19, 20; Psalm 15:5; Proverbs 28:8; Jeremiah 15:10)

7) How did Nehemiah respond upon hearing this news?

_____

_____

_____

Circle every verb (that is, action word) connected with Nehemiah in this chapter.

8) What behavior did Nehemiah demand of his wealthy neighbors? How did he insure that they would keep their word?

_____

_____

_____

(verses to consider: Numbers 30; Deuteronomy 23:21–23; Psalm 66:13–15; 116:18; Ecclesiastes 5:5–6)

Cross Reference

Read Jeremiah 22:13–19.

13 *"Woe to him who builds his house by unrighteousness*
   And his chambers by injustice,
   Who uses his neighbor's service without wages
   And gives him nothing for his work,
14 *"Who says, 'I will build myself a wide house with spacious chambers,*
   And cut out windows for it,
   Paneling it with cedar
   And painting it with vermilion.'
15 *"Shall you reign because you enclose yourself in cedar?*
   Did not your father eat and drink,
   And do justice and righteousness?
   Then it was well with him.
16 *He judged the cause of the poor and needy;*
   Then it was well.
   Was not this knowing Me?" says the LORD.
17 *"Yet your eyes and your heart are for nothing but your covetousness,*
   For shedding innocent blood,
   And practicing oppression and violence."
18 *Therefore thus says the LORD concerning Jehoiakim the son of Josiah, king of Judah:*
   "They shall not lament for him,
   Saying, 'Alas, my brother!' or 'Alas, my sister!'
   They shall not lament for him,
   Saying, 'Alas, master!' or 'Alas, his glory!'
19 *He shall be buried with the burial of a donkey,*
   Dragged and cast out beyond the gates of Jerusalem.

Exploring the Meaning

9) What did God say to King Jehoiakim because of his greed and mistreatment of the people of God? How was his behavior different from that of his father, King Josiah (vv. 15–16)?

_____

_____

_____

10) Read Proverbs 19:23. How does the fear of the Lord prevent us from sinning? How did the fear of the Lord keep Nehemiah from sinning?

_____

_____

(verses to consider: 2 Chronicles 19:7; Psalm 34:11; Proverbs 1:7; 10:27; 14:27; Acts 9:31)

11) Read Luke 22:25–27. What did Jesus say here about leadership? What evidence do you see in Nehemiah 5 that Nehemiah lived out the principles in these verses?

_____

_____

Summing Up...

"Our society replaces people with things, conversation with entertainment. By so doing, we have lost the simple joys of life, which center on relationships, the essence of Christian fellowship. Material things can pull believers away from those vital relationships with God and others."—*John MacArthur*

Reflecting on the Text

12) Thomas Merton has written, "To consider persons and events and situa-

tions only in the light of their effect upon myself is to live on the doorstep of hell."

Consider your own track record of dealing with people. Are you (like the rich Jews of Nehemiah's day) an opportunist who mainly thinks about material things-how you can get ahead, get more stuff, and prosper? Or (like Nehemiah) are you a servant who uses your gifts, resources, time, and treasure to bless others and build them up? How can you be more like Nehemiah?

_____

_____

13) What needs to change in your life in the area of money, specifically giving? What financial need (of an individual or in your church) can you meet today?

_____

_____

14) Nehemiah saw a social problem, an injustice, and he became agitated enough to do something about it. What social concerns do you have today? What is something you will commit to do this week in an attempt to effect change to the glory of God?

_____

_____

Recording Your Thoughts

_____

_____

_____

For further study, see the following passages:

Genesis 13:8	Exodus 32	Leviticus 25
Deuteronomy 24:10–13	1 Kings 4:22	1 Kings 18:19
Proverbs 16:32	Ecclesiastes 5:11	Matthew 10:14
Luke 19:1–10	Acts 3:51	Ephesians 4:26

Mission Accomplished!

Nehemiah 6:1–19

Opening Thought

1) Were you ever bullied or picked on as a child? What was the experience like? What eventually happened?

_____

_____

_____

_____

2) Describe the most intense spiritual warfare you've ever experienced. What were you trying to do? How were you being thwarted?

_____

_____

_____

_____

3) List two or three accomplishments in your life that: (a) seemed initially to be impossible; and (b) ultimately were extremely gratifying.

_____

_____

_____

_____

Background of the Passage

Baseball Hall-of-Famer Yogi Berra is credited with coining the famous phrase, "It's not over till it's over." This statement is quite accurate in describing the relentless opposition of Nehemiah's enemies. Having failed to stop Nehemiah's wall-building effort by open military engagement (see 4:13–15), Sanballat, Tobiah, and Geshem resorted to new tactics.

An invitation to meet in the plains of Ono (v. 2) was rightfully discerned by Nehemiah to be a trap. He refused the offer. Shortly thereafter, an open letter was sent (v. 5). Such an unsealed communique was not only a sign of disrespect and open criticism, but also suggested the information therein was public knowledge. The goal of this document was to intimidate Nehemiah into stopping his wall-building work. Nehemiah refused to budge.

Next the evil triumvirate accused Nehemiah of plotting to declare himself king. Artaxerxes of Persia had commissioned the rebuilding of the wall, based on his relationship of trust with Nehemiah. Once the project was accomplished, the king expected Nehemiah to return to Susa. Allegations that Nehemiah was fortifying the city so that he might be made king would seriously violate the Persian king's trust, if not create a war. But not even this slic ploy could coerce Nehemiah into meeting with his murderous enemies.

Having failed to intimidate Nehemiah into stopping the work and coming to a meeting, his enemies decided to try trickery from within. They hired a false prophet (v. 12), Shemaiah, to lure Nehemiah into the Holy Place in the temp for refuge from a murder plot. To enter and shut himself in the Holy Place would have been a desecration of the house of God and would have caused people to question his reverence for God.

Nehemiah wisely perceived that "God had not sent him at all." Instead of caving in to pressure or fear, Nehemiah prayed and continued his work.

The result? Verse 15: "So the wall was finished . . . in fifty-two days." The lesson? The faithful God of heaven and earth rewards the diligence and faith fulness of His servants.

Bible Passage

Read 6:1–19, noting the key words and definitions to the right of the passag

Nehemiah 6:1–19:

¹ *Now it happened when Sanballat, Tobiah, Geshem the Arab, and the rest of our enemies heard that I had rebuilt the wall, and that there were no breaks left in it (though at that time I had not hung the doors in the gates),*

² *that Sanballat and Geshem sent to me, saying, "Come, let us meet together among the villages in the plain of Ono." But they thought to do me harm.*

³ *So I sent messengers to them, saying, "I am doing a great work, so that I cannot come down. Why should the work cease while I leave it and go down to you?"*

⁴ *But they sent me this message four times, and I answered them in the same manner.*

⁵ *Then Sanballat sent his servant to me as before, the fifth time, with an open letter in his hand.*

⁶ *In it was written: It is reported among the nations, and Geshem says, that you and the Jews plan to rebel; therefore, according to these rumors, you are rebuilding the wall, that you may be their king.*

⁷ *And you have also appointed prophets to proclaim concerning you at Jerusalem, saying, "There is a king in Judah!" Now these matters will be reported to the king. So come, therefore, and let us consult together.*

⁸ *Then I sent to him, saying, "No such things as you say are being done, but you invent them in your own heart."*

⁹ *For they all were trying to make us afraid, saying, "Their hands will be weakened in the work, and it will not be done."*

Now therefore, O God, strengthen my hands.

¹⁰ *Afterward I came to the house of Shemaiah the son of Delaiah, the son of Mehetabel, who was a secret informer; and he said, "Let us meet together in the house of God, within the temple, and let us close the doors of the temple, for they*

sent to me (v. 2)—This suggests either a letter or an oral message delivered by messenger to Nehemiah.

plain of Ono (v. 2)—located south of Joppa on the western extremity of Judah along the sea-coast

So I sent messengers (v. 3)—Because he knew they were luring him into a trap, he sent representatives, who themselves might have been killed or imprisoned for ransom.

open letter (v. 5)—Official letters were typically rolled up and sealed with an official signet by the letter's sender or one of his assisting officials.

It is reported among the nations (v. 6)—The letter suggested that Nehemiah's intent to revolt was common knowledge which would get back to the king of Persia if he didn't come to the requested conference.

you and the Jews plan to rebel (v. 6)—This information would have brought Persian troops against the Jews had it been true. Even though Judah had a reputation for breaking its allegiances with its overlord kings, on this occasion that was not the case.

rebuilding the wall, that you may be their king (v. 6)—This was an attempt to intimidate Nehemiah with the idea that a wedge was to be driven between Nehemiah and Artaxerxes so that Nehemiah would come to the meeting with those enemies-a meeting that would have featured his death.

appointed prophets to proclaim (v. 7)—If there were such prophets, Sanballat actually hired them to feed incorrect information

are coming to kill you; indeed, at night they will come to kill you."

11 *And I said, "Should such a man as I flee? And who is there such as I who would go into the temple to save his life? I will not go in!"*

12 *Then I perceived that God had not sent him at all, but that he pronounced this prophecy against me because Tobiah and Sanballat had hired him.*

13 *For this reason he was hired, that I should be afraid and act that way and sin, so that they might have cause for an evil report, that they might reproach me.*

14 *My God, remember Tobiah and Sanballat, according to these their works, and the prophetess Noadiah and the rest of the prophets who would have made me afraid.*

15 *So the wall was finished on the twenty-fifth day of Elul, in fifty-two days.*

16 *And it happened, when all our enemies heard of it, and all the nations around us saw these things, that they were very disheartened in their own eyes; for they perceived that this work was done by our God.*

17 *Also in those days the nobles of Judah sent many letters to Tobiah, and the letters of Tobiah came to them.*

18 *For many in Judah were pledged to him, because he was the son-in-law of Shechaniah the son of Arah, and his son Jehohanan had married the daughter of Meshullam the son of Berechiah.*

19 *Also they reported his good deeds before me, and reported my words to him. Tobiah sent letters to frighten me.*

generating the false rumor (see 6:10–14). By dispatching such prophets to make public proclamations that Nehemiah had made himself king, the Persian imperial rule would have appeared to be supplanted.

secret informer (v. 10)—Shemaiah was the son of a priest who was an intimate friend of Nehemiah. This plan would give them grounds to raise an evil report against Nehemiah, who was not a priest and had no right to go into the Holy Place (see 6:13). It could also make the people question his courage (v. 11). Other disloyal Jews included (1) the nobles (3:5; 6:17); (2) Jews who lived near Sanballat (4:12); (3) Noadiah (6:14); (4) Meshullam (6:17–19); (5) Eliashib (13:4, 7); and (6) the high priest's grandson (13:28).

the house of God (v. 10)—This is a frequently used name for the temple (see 8:16; 10:32–39; 11:11, 16, 22; 12:40; 13:4, 7, 9, 11, 14).

Elul (v. 15)—August/September, 445 B.C.; since the project lasted 52 days, it must have commenced on the fourth of Ab (July/August) 445 B.C.

this work was done by our God (v. 16)—While modern readers might be tempted to exalt the leadership qualities which brought the work to completion, Nehemiah's conclusion was seen through the eyes of his enemies; that is, God works through faithful people, but it is God who works. This is a change from the attitudes indicated in 4:1 and 5:9.

the nobles of Judah sent many letters to Tobiah (vv. 17–19)—Nehemiah added a footnote that in the days of building the wall, the nobles of Judah who refused to work (3:5) were in alliance and correspondence with Tobiah because, although his ancestors were Ammonites (2:19), he had married into a respectable Jewish family. Shemaiah was from the family of Arah (Ezra 2:5); his son Jehohanan was the son-in-law of Meshullam who shared in the work of building (Neh. 3:4, 30). According to 13:4, the high priest, Eliashib, was related to Tobiah (which is a Jewish name). The meddling of these nobles, by trying to play both sides through reports to Tobiah and to Nehemiah (v. 19), only widened the breach as Tobiah escalated efforts to frighten the governor.

Understanding the Text

4) What prompted Nehemiah's enemies to summon him to a meeting? What was their intention? What was their overall objective? (hint: see verse 9)

_____

_____

_____

5) Underline every response of Nehemiah to his enemies' suggestions. How did Nehemiah respond to their offers and threats?

_____

_____

_____

6) What did Shemaiah attempt to convince Nehemiah to do? Why was Nehemiah unwilling?

_____

_____

_____

7) What role did prayer play in Nehemiah's defense against these enemy attacks?

_____

_____

_____

(verses to consider: Ephesians 6:18–20; Philippians 4:6, 7; 1 Timothy 2:1–3)

8) What illegitimate actions were the nobles of Judah guilty of?

_____

_____

_____

Cross Reference

Read Ephesians 6:10–18.

¹⁰ *Finally, my brethren, be strong in the Lord and in the power of His might.*
¹¹ *Put on the whole armor of God, that you may be able to stand against the wiles of the devil.*
¹² *For we do not wrestle against flesh and blood, but against principalities, against powers, against the rulers of the darkness of this age, against spiritual hosts of wickedness in the heavenly places.*
¹³ *Therefore take up the whole armor of God, that you may be able to withstand in the evil day, and having done all, to stand.*
¹⁴ *Stand therefore, having girded your waist with truth, having put on the breast-plate of righteousness,*
¹⁵ *and having shod your feet with the preparation of the gospel of peace;*
¹⁶ *above all, taking the shield of faith with which you will be able to quench all the fiery darts of the wicked one.*
¹⁷ *And take the helmet of salvation, and the sword of the Spirit, which is the word of God;*
¹⁸ *praying always with all prayer and supplication in the Spirit, being watchful to this end with all perseverance and supplication for all the saints.*

Exploring the Meaning

9) Why is it often hard to remember that behind our earthly conflicts is the cosmic war described by Paul in Ephesians 6?

_____

_____

_____

10) Read Acts 21:10–14. How did Paul respond to the fact that there were men who wanted to take his life?

_____

_____

_____

11) Read Deuteronomy 13:1–5. What does this passage say about testing those who claim to be speaking God's Word to us? Why shouldn't we listen to everyone who dispenses religious counsel (see Nehemiah 6:10–12)?

_____

_____

_____

Summing Up...

"In the great spiritual warfare in which we do battle, we are only called to resist and to stand firm. . . . James says, 'Resist the devil and he will flee from you' (James 4:7). Peter counsels us to 'be of sober spirit, be on the alert. Your adversary, the devil, prowls about like a roaring lion, seeking someone to devour. But resist him, firm in our faith' (1 Peter 5:8–9). The greatest joys come in the greatest victories, and the greatest victories come from the greatest battles-when they are fought in the power and with the armor of the Lord."—*John MacArthur*

Reflecting on the Text

12) Jesus spoke about "turning the other cheek" (Luke 6:29), and yet Nehemiah in no way yielded to his opponents. When is it appropriate to resist our enemies? To fight back?

_____

_____

_____

13) What insights does this passage shed on the truth of spiritual warfare? On the persistence of the enemy?

_____

_____

_____

(verses to consider: John 8:42–44; 10:10; 2 Corinthians 11:3, 13–15; 1 Peter 5:8–9)

14) What kind of intense opposition are you facing in your walk right now? How can you apply the lessons you've learned here in Nehemiah 6?

_____

_____

_____

15) Write down two specific, concrete actions you can take to show support to your pastor this week. (He is, no doubt, under attack—fighting various spiritual battles; your encouragement will mean a great deal!)

_____

_____

_____

Recording Your Thoughts

_____

_____

_____

For further study, see the following passages:

Exodus 21:13, 14	Numbers 18:7	1 Kings 1:50–53
2 Chronicles 26:16–21	Ezra 4	Proverbs 28:4
Isaiah 8:20	Jeremiah 9:4	Luke 23:1–5
John 10:12–13		

Rebuilding the People Inside the Walls!

Nehemiah 7:1–73

Opening Thought

1) Why do you think genealogy is such a popular hobby?

_____

_____

_____

2) How can we know when a project is truly finished? What are the signs?

_____

_____

_____

3) What projects do you engage in that are never really finished? Is this more challenging for you or more frustrating? Why?

_____

_____

_____

4) Which do you prefer: working with people or working on a task alone? What are the special challenges of working with people?

_____

_____

_____

_____

Background of the Passage

Consider the beautiful house occupied by a terribly dysfunctional family. Is this a healthy home? Of course not! Consider the exploding megachurch with the multi-million dollar facility. Is such obvious popularity and growth a reliable indicator that God is pleased? Not necessarily.

Our foolish culture often makes the mistake of assuming that if a thing looks good, it must actually be good. Fallen people in a fallen world will always struggle with this tendency to equate appearance with substance. If we're not careful we can become self-satisfied and complacent when our lives merely look good on the surface. But without internal health and strength, without addressing the deeper issues and hard-to-see problems, no work is finished. We must take care not to confuse externals with internals. Addressing our physical/material needs alone will not automatically take care of our spiritual deficiencies.

This was the situation in Jerusalem immediately following the rebuilding of the walls under Nehemiah. Perhaps the people were ready to declare the work finished. It is likely they were tired. They might have congratulated themselves for finishing a difficult and complicated construction project, set down their tools, and said, "Now, let's get back to a normal life."

But the work was not finished and Nehemiah knew it. A city is more than bricks and mortar, walls and gates. A city is people. And if Jerusalem was going to become the city God intended, the city to be visited by Messiah, it was important to immediately address the broken-down condition of the hearts of the people

Nehemiah 7 reveals the crucial foundation laid by Nehemiah for a spiritual revival that God would soon engineer through the leadership of Ezra.

Bible Passage

Read 7:1–73, noting the key words and definitions to the right of the passage.

Nehemiah 7:1–73:
¹ *Then it was, when the wall was built and I had hung the doors, when the gatekeepers, the singers, and the Levites had been appointed,*

64

² *that I gave the charge of Jerusalem to my brother Hanani, and Hananiah the leader of the citadel, for he was a faithful man and feared God more than many.*

³ *And I said to them, "Do not let the gates of Jerusalem be opened until the sun is hot; and while they stand guard, let them shut and bar the doors; and appoint guards from among the inhabitants of Jerusalem, one at his watch station and another in front of his own house."*

⁴ *Now the city was large and spacious, but the people in it were few, and the houses were not rebuilt.*

⁵ *Then my God put it into my heart to gather the nobles, the rulers, and the people, that they might be registered by genealogy. And I found a register of the genealogy of those who had come up in the first return, and found written in it:*

⁶ *These are the people of the province who came back from the captivity, of those who had been carried away, whom Nebuchadnezzar the king of Babylon had carried away, and who returned to Jerusalem and Judah, everyone to his city.*

⁷ *Those who came with Zerubbabel were Jeshua, Nehemiah, Azariah, Raamiah, Nahamani, Mordecai, Bilshan, Mispereth, Bigvai, Nehum, and Baanah.*

The number of the men of the people of Israel:

⁸ *the sons of Parosh, two thousand one hundred and seventy-two;*

⁹ *the sons of Shephatiah, three hundred and seventy-two;*

¹⁰ *the sons of Arah, six hundred and fifty-two;*

¹¹ *the sons of Pahath-Moab, of the sons of Jeshua and Joab, two thousand eight hundred and eighteen;*

¹² *the sons of Elam, one thousand two hundred and fifty-four;*

¹³ *the sons of Zattu, eight hundred and forty-five;*

¹⁴ *the sons of Zaccai, seven hundred and sixty;*

¹⁵ *the sons of Binnui, six hundred and forty-eight;*

¹⁶ *the sons of Bebai, six hundred and twenty-eight;*

¹⁷ *the sons of Azgad, two thousand three hundred and twenty-two;*

Hanani (v. 2)—see 1:2

the citadel (v. 2)—see note on 2:8

do not let the gates . . . be opened . . . (v. 3)—In the ancient Near East, it was customary to open the city gates at sunrise and close them at sunset. Nehemiah recommended that this not be done, because of the hostility of the enemies. Rather the gates were to be kept shut until well into the heat of the morning when everyone was up and active. When the gates were shut, they were to be guarded by sentinels at watch stations and in front of their own vulnerable homes (v. 4).

my God put it into my heart (v. 5)—Throughout the book, Nehemiah claimed the hand of God was at work in all circumstances (see 2:8, 18; 6:16; 7:5).

I found a register (vv. 5–6)—Nehemiah discovered a register of the people made by Ezra in Babylon before the first group returned, a listing of the people who had come with Zerubbabel.

These are the people . . . who came back from the captivity (v. 6)—Nehemiah gave the list of those in the first return from Persia to Jerusalem under Zerubbabel in 538 B.C. Minor discrepancies are possibly due to Ezra's listing those who intended to depart, while Nehemiah listed those who actually arrived; or some other unknown reason.

¹⁸ *the sons of Adonikam, six hundred and sixty-seven;*

¹⁹ *the sons of Bigvai, two thousand and sixty-seven;*

²⁰ *the sons of Adin, six hundred and fifty-five;*

²¹ *the sons of Ater of Hezekiah, ninety-eight;*

²² *the sons of Hashum, three hundred and twenty-eight;*

²³ *the sons of Bezai, three hundred and twenty-four;*

²⁴ *the sons of Hariph, one hundred and twelve;*

²⁵ *the sons of Gibeon, ninety-five;*

²⁶ *the men of Bethlehem and Netophah, one hundred and eighty-eight;*

²⁷ *the men of Anathoth, one hundred and twenty-eight;*

²⁸ *the men of Beth Azmaveth, forty-two;*

²⁹ *the men of Kirjath Jearim, Chephirah, and Beeroth, seven hundred and forty-three;*

³⁰ *the men of Ramah and Geba, six hundred and twenty-one;*

³¹ *the men of Michmas, one hundred and twenty-two;*

³² *the men of Bethel and Ai, one hundred and twenty-three;*

³³ *the men of the other Nebo, fifty-two;*

³⁴ *the sons of the other Elam, one thousand two hundred and fifty-four;*

³⁵ *the sons of Harim, three hundred and twenty;*

³⁶ *the sons of Jericho, three hundred and forty-five;*

³⁷ *the sons of Lod, Hadid, and Ono, seven hundred and twenty-one;*

³⁸ *the sons of Senaah, three thousand nine hundred and thirty.*

³⁹ *The priests: the sons of Jedaiah, of the house of Jeshua, nine hundred and seventy-three;*

⁴⁰ *the sons of Immer, one thousand and fifty-two;*

⁴¹ *the sons of Pashhur, one thousand two hundred and forty-seven;*

⁴² *the sons of Harim, one thousand and seventeen.*

⁴³ *The Levites: the sons of Jeshua, of Kadmiel, and of the sons of Hodevah, seventy-four.*

⁴⁴ *The singers: the sons of Asaph, one hundred and forty-eight.*

⁴⁵ *The gatekeepers: the sons of Shallum, the sons of*

Ater, the sons of Talmon, the sons of Akkub, the sons of Hatita, the sons of Shobai, one hundred and thirty-eight.

46 The Nethinim: the sons of Ziha, the sons of Hasupha, the sons of Tabbaoth,

47 the sons of Keros, the sons of Sia, the sons of Padon,

48 the sons of Lebana, the sons of Hagaba, the sons of Salmai,

49 the sons of Hanan, the sons of Giddel, the sons of Gahar,

50 the sons of Reaiah, the sons of Rezin, the sons of Nekoda,

51 the sons of Gazzam, the sons of Uzza, the sons of Paseah,

52 the sons of Besai, the sons of Meunim, the sons of Nephishesim,

53 the sons of Bakbuk, the sons of Hakupha, the sons of Harhur,

54 the sons of Bazlith, the sons of Mehida, the sons of Harsha,

55 the sons of Barkos, the sons of Sisera, the sons of Tamah,

56 the sons of Neziah, and the sons of Hatipha.

57 The sons of Solomon's servants: the sons of Sotai, the sons of Sophereth, the sons of Perida,

58 the sons of Jaala, the sons of Darkon, the sons of Giddel,

59 the sons of Shephatiah, the sons of Hattil, the sons of Pochereth of Zebaim, and the sons of Amon.

60 All the Nethinim, and the sons of Solomon's servants, were three hundred and ninety-two.

61 And these were the ones who came up from Tel Melah, Tel Harsha, Cherub, Addon, and Immer, but they could not identify their father's house nor their lineage, whether they were of Israel:

62 the sons of Delaiah, the sons of Tobiah, the sons of Nekoda, six hundred and forty-two;

63 and of the priests: the sons of Habaiah, the sons of Koz, the sons of Barzillai, who took a wife of the daughters of Barzillai the Gileadite, and was called by their name.

64 *These sought their listing among those who were registered by genealogy, but it was not found; therefore they were excluded from the priesthood as defiled.*

65 *And the governor said to them that they should not eat of the most holy things till a priest could consult with the Urim and Thummim.*

66 *Altogether the whole assembly was forty-two thousand three hundred and sixty,*

67 *besides their male and female servants, of whom there were seven thousand three hundred and thirty-seven; and they had two hundred and forty-five men and women singers.*

68 *Their horses were seven hundred and thirty-six, their mules two hundred and forty-five,*

69 *their camels four hundred and thirty-five, and donkeys six thousand seven hundred and twenty.*

70 *And some of the heads of the fathers' houses gave to the work. The governor gave to the treasury one thousand gold drachmas, fifty basins, and five hundred and thirty priestly garments.*

71 *Some of the heads of the fathers' houses gave to the treasury of the work twenty thousand gold drachmas, and two thousand two hundred silver minas.*

72 *And that which the rest of the people gave was twenty thousand gold drachmas, two thousand silver minas, and sixty-seven priestly garments.*

73 *So the priests, the Levites, the gatekeepers, the singers, some of the people, the Nethinim, and all Israel dwelt in their cities.*

When the seventh month came, the children of Israel were in their cities.

consult with the Urim and Thummim (v. 65)—one of the methods used to discern the will of God on a specific matter

seventh month (v. 73)—This refers to the month of Tishri (Sept./Oct.) 445 B.C., less than one week after completing the walls (see 6:15). The Feast of Tabernacles usually began on the fifteenth day (see 6:15 with Lev. 23:33–4)—but here it began on the second (see 8:13)—and it was a feast to which the whole nation was called. Usually the Feast of Trumpets occurred on the first day (see Lev. 23:23–25).

Understanding the Text

5) Why did Nehemiah give special instructions about guards and locked gates?

_____

_____

_____

_____

_____

6) How was Hananiah described (verse 2)?

_____

_____

_____

_____

_____

7) What motivated Nehemiah to organize a city-wide genealogical research project? What happened to those who could not verify their priestly roots (vv. 64–65)?

_____

_____

_____

_____

_____

Cross Reference

Read Acts 6:1–7.

1 *Now in those days, when the number of the disciples was multiplying, there arose a complaint against the Hebrews by the Hellenists, because their widows were neglected in the daily distribution.*
2 *Then the twelve summoned the multitude of the disciples and said, "It is not desirable that we should leave the word of God and serve tables.*
3 *"Therefore, brethren, seek out from among you seven men of good reputation, full of the Holy Spirit and wisdom, whom we may appoint over this business;*
4 *"but we will give ourselves continually to prayer and to the ministry of the word."*

5 *And the saying pleased the whole multitude. And they chose Stephen, a man full of faith and the Holy Spirit, and Philip, Prochorus, Nicanor, Timon, Parmenas, and Nicolas, a proselyte from Antioch,*

6 *whom they set before the apostles; and when they had prayed, they laid hands on them.*

7 *Then the word of God spread, and the number of the disciples multiplied greatly in Jerusalem, and a great many of the priests were obedient to the faith.*

Exploring the Meaning

8) What criteria did the apostles use in choosing servants for the early church? How is this similar to the method Nehemiah followed in choosing leaders for Jerusalem?

_____

_____

_____

_____

_____

9) Hananiah was chosen for leadership because of his character. Read 1 Timothy 3:2–7. What character qualities does Paul say are necessary for leadership in the church? How does this compare with the world's usual criteria for leadership?

_____

_____

_____

_____

_____

10) Read Psalm 137. Though the Israelites did not sing much during their years of exile, Nehemiah, in this chapter, gave special instructions that included singers (vv. 1, 44, 67, 73). Why is worship such an important part of building a strong community of faith?

_____

_____

_____

_____

_____

(verses to consider: 1 Chronicles 15:16; 2 Chronicles 5:13; 29:28; Nehemiah 10:28, 39)

Summing Up...

"The most important qualities leaders can demonstrate are not intelligence, a forceful personality, glibness, diligence, vision, administrative skills, decisiveness, courage, humor, tact, or any other similar natural attribute. Those all play a part, but the most desirable quality for any leader is integrity."
—*John MacArthur*

Recording Your Thoughts

11) In light of Nehemiah's example, what criteria should we follow in choosing leaders? Why is it so critical that we choose church leaders carefully?

_____

_____

_____

_____

12) How could you develop the kind of integrity and character that would make you eligible for a position of leadership?

_____

_____

_____

_____

_____

13) What are one or two situations in which you sense God putting it into your heart to do a certain thing? How can you confirm that this is the will of God?

_____

_____

_____

_____

_____

Recording Your Thoughts

_____

_____

_____

_____

_____

_____

_____

_____

_____

_____

For further study, see the following passages:

Proverbs 29:15	Ezra 2:1--64	Ezra 2:68–70
Psalm 11:3	Luke 10:20	John 3:1–18
Romans 14:7–12	Hebrews 11	1 John 5:9–13

The Power of the Word

Opening Thought

1) What is your favorite holiday or special occasion to celebrate? Why?

_____

_____

_____

_____

2) Describe the most recent occasion during which you felt completely overcome by joy. What made you feel such deep gladness?

_____

_____

_____

_____

3) On a scale of 1–10 (with 1 meaning "I never do that!" and 10 meaning "I do that almost non-stop!") evaluate your relationship to the written Word of God in the following areas.

_____ Hearing the Bible preached or taught
_____ Reading the Scripture
_____ Studying God's Word
_____ Understanding the Bible
_____ Memorizing the Word of God
_____ Meditating on Scripture
_____ Obeying the Word of God
_____ Teaching God's truth to others

Background of the Passage

Europe is legendary for its beautiful cathedrals. The problem with many of these magnificent structures is that, while they possess physical grandeur, they are not inhabited by congregations that are spiritually vibrant. In reality, most of these edifices are nothing more than museums visited by gawking tourists. This phenomenon should remind us that the spiritual life is about internals, not externals.

The Old Testament Book of Nehemiah details the extraordinary accomplishment of the Jewish people, under the capable leadership of Governor Nehemiah, of rebuilding the walls of Jerusalem in only 52 days (chapters 1–6). But the remainder of the book (chapters 7–13) tells of an even more significant process-the spiritual renovation of the people who lived behind the walls.

Following the completion of the walls in the face of great opposition (chapters 3–6) and the genealogical "census" of the inhabitants of Jerusalem (chapter 7), a great convocation was held. In effect, Nehemiah called for a "Bible conference," with Ezra the scribe as the special speaker.

At the rebuilt Water Gate, God's law (probably the Book of Deuteronomy) was read and explained to a great assembly. The initial effect was that the people were convicted and grief-stricken regarding their failure to keep God's law. But with the help of the Levites, Nehemiah convinced the people of God's mercy and forgiveness. Consequently a profound sense of joy permeated the people of God. With great gladness, they celebrated the Feast of Tabernacles.

The result? Jerusalem was not only a city with an impressive new wall; it was a city populated by people with a new spirit and a new resolve to live in light of God's Word!

Bible Passage

Read 8:1–18, noting the key words and definitions to the right of the passage.

Nehemiah 8:1–18:

¹ *Now all the people gathered together as one man in the open square that was in front of the Water Gate; and they told Ezra the scribe to bring the*

the Book . . . the Law (vv. 1–2)—In response to the people's request, Ezra brought the law of the Lord, which he had set his heart to study, practice, and teach

Book of the Law of Moses, which the LORD had commanded Israel.

2 So Ezra the priest brought the Law before the assembly of men and women and all who could hear with understanding on the first day of the seventh month.

3 Then he read from it in the open square that was in front of the Water Gate from morning until midday, before the men and women and those who could understand; and the ears of all the people were attentive to the Book of the Law.

4 So Ezra the scribe stood on a platform of wood which they had made for the purpose; and beside him, at his right hand, stood Mattithiah, Shema, Anaiah, Urijah, Hilkiah, and Maaseiah; and at his left hand Pedaiah, Mishael, Malchijah, Hashum, Hashbadana, Zechariah, and Meshullam.

5 And Ezra opened the book in the sight of all the people, for he was standing above all the people; and when he opened it, all the people stood up.

6 And Ezra blessed the LORD, the great God. Then all the people answered, "Amen, Amen!" while lifting up their hands. And they bowed their heads and worshiped the LORD with their faces to the ground.

7 Also Jeshua, Bani, Sherebiah, Jamin, Akkub, Shabbethai, Hodijah, Maaseiah, Kelita, Azariah, Jozabad, Hanan, Pelaiah, and the Levites, helped the people to understand the Law; and the people stood in their place.

8 So they read distinctly from the book, in the Law of God; and they gave the sense, and helped them to understand the reading.

9 And Nehemiah, who was the governor, Ezra the priest and scribe, and the Levites who taught the people said to all the people, "This day is holy to the LORD your God; do not mourn nor weep." For all the people wept, when they heard the words of the Law.

10 Then he said to them, "Go your way, eat the fat,

to the people (see Ezra 7:10). At this time, the law was a scroll, as opposed to a text consisting of bound pages. Such a reading was required every 7 years at the Feast of Tabernacles, even though it had been neglected since the Babylonian captivity until this occasion.

the Water Gate (v. 1)—see note on 3:26

Ezra (v. 1)—This is the first mention of Ezra in the Book of Nehemiah, though he had been ministering in Jerusalem since 458 B.C. (see Ezra 7:1–10:44).

read . . . understand (v. 3)— Here is the general summary of the event of reading and explaining the Scripture from daybreak to noon, a period of at least 6 hours (more detail is added in vv. 4–8).

platform . . . beside him (v. 4) —The platform was big enough to hold fourteen people for the long hours of reading and explaining (v. 8). The men, probably priests, stood with Nehemiah to show agreement.

stood up (v. 5)—In respect at the reading of God's Word, as though they were in the presence of God Himself, the people stood for all the hours of the exposition.

blessed the Lord (v. 6)—This was a praise befitting the reading. In a synagogue, the reading is preceded by a benediction. The response of "Amen, Amen" was an affirmation of what Ezra prayed.

Also Jeshua . . . Pelaiah, and the Levites, helped the people to understand the Law (vv. 7–8)—Some of the Levites assisted Ezra with the people's understanding of the Scripture by reading and explaining it.

drink the sweet, and send portions to those for whom nothing is prepared; for this day is holy to our LORD. Do not sorrow, for the joy of the LORD is your strength."

11 So the Levites quieted all the people, saying, "Be still, for the day is holy; do not be grieved."

12 And all the people went their way to eat and drink, to send portions and rejoice greatly, because they understood the words that were declared to them.

13 Now on the second day the heads of the fathers' houses of all the people, with the priests and Levites, were gathered to Ezra the scribe, in order to understand the words of the Law.

14 And they found written in the Law, which the LORD had commanded by Moses, that the children of Israel should dwell in booths during the feast of the seventh month,

15 and that they should announce and proclaim in all their cities and in Jerusalem, saying, "Go out to the mountain, and bring olive branches, branches of oil trees, myrtle branches, palm branches, and branches of leafy trees, to make booths, as it is written."

16 Then the people went out and brought them and made themselves booths, each one on the roof of his house, or in their courtyards or the courts of the house of God, and in the open square of the Water Gate and in the open square of the Gate of Ephraim.

17 So the whole assembly of those who had returned from the captivity made booths and sat under the booths; for since the days of Joshua the son of Nun until that day the children of Israel had not done so. And there was very great gladness.

18 Also day by day, from the first day until the last day, he read from the Book of the Law of God. And they kept the feast seven days; and on the eighth day there was a sacred assembly, according to the prescribed manner.

gave the sense (v. 8)—This may have involved translation for people who were only Aramaic speakers in exile, but more likely it means "to break down" the text into its parts so that the people could understand it. This was an exposition or explanation of the meaning and not just translation.

helped them to understand the reading (v. 8)—In this act of instruction, Ezra's personal commitment to study the law, practice it in his own life, and then teach it (Ezra 7:10) was reflected.

governor (v. 9)—see note on 5:14

Ezra the priest (v. 9)—see Ezra 7:11, 12, 21; 10:10, 16

wept, when they heard the words of the Law (v. 9)— When they heard and understood God's law, they understood their violations of it. Not tears of joy, but penitent sorrow (8:10) came forth as they were grieved by conviction (8:11) over the distressing manifestations of sin in transgressing the Lord's commands and the consequent punishments they had suffered in their captivity.

the joy of the Lord is your strength (vv. 10–12)—The event called for a holy day of worship to prepare them for the hard days ahead (see 12:43), so they were encouraged to rejoice. The words they had heard did remind them that God punishes sin, but also that God blesses obedience. That was reason to celebrate. They had not been utterly destroyed as a nation, in spite of their sin, and were, by God's grace, on the brink of a new beginning. That called for celebration.

in order to understand the words of the Law (v. 13)—The smaller group that gathered to Ezra consisted of those who had teaching responsibilities: the heads of the father's houses to their families, and the priests and Levites to the general population in the community (Mal. 2:6–7).

they should announce and proclaim (vv. 15–16)—Proclamations such as this carried the authority of the administration represented by leaders such as Nehemiah, who was the governor, and Ezra, the priest and scribe (8:9) who had been used to reestablish the city, its worship, and its social life. The people responded to their directive.

Water Gate (v. 16)—see notes on 3:26; 12:37

Gate of Ephraim (v. 16)—This is believed to have been near the Old Gate (see 3:6; 12:39).

since the days of Joshua . . . very great gladness (v. 17)—Tabernacles had been celebrated since Joshua (2 Chron. 7:8–10; Ezra 3:4), but not with such joy.

Also (v. 18)—This was more than was required and arose from the exuberant zeal of the people.

Understanding the Text

4) Why is it significant that the people congregated at the Water Gate (v. 1)?

_____

_____

_____

5) Who were all the men on the platform with Ezra and what was their job description? Why is this important?

_____

_____

_____

Underline each occurrence of the word "understand" or "understanding" in this chapter.

6) What attitude did the people of Israel have toward the Scripture? (8:3, 6, 9, 17)

_____

_____

_____

(verses to consider: 1 Thessalonians 2:13; 2 Timothy 3:16–17; Hebrews 4:12)

7) On the second day of the convocation, how did the people react to the rediscovered instructions regarding the Feast of Tabernacles (8:16–18)?

_____

_____

_____

(verses to consider: Leviticus 23:23–44; Numbers 29:12–38; Deuteronomy 16:13–17; Zechariah 14:4, 9, 16–20)

Cross Reference

Read Psalm 119:1–48.

¹ *Blessed are the undefiled in the way,*
  Who walk in the law of the Lord!
² *Blessed are those who keep His testimonies,*
  Who seek Him with the whole heart!
³ *They also do no iniquity;*
  They walk in His ways.
⁴ *You have commanded us*
  To keep Your precepts diligently.
⁵ *Oh, that my ways were directed*
  To keep Your statutes!
⁶ *Then I would not be ashamed,*
  When I look into all Your commandments.
⁷ *I will praise You with uprightness of heart,*
  When I learn Your righteous judgments.
⁸ *I will keep Your statutes;*
  Oh, do not forsake me utterly!
⁹ *How can a young man cleanse his way?*
  By taking heed according to Your word.
¹⁰ *With my whole heart I have sought You;*
  Oh, let me not wander from Your commandments!
¹¹ *Your word I have hidden in my heart,*
  That I might not sin against You!
¹² *Blessed are You, O Lord!*
  Teach me Your statutes!

13 *With my lips I have declared*
   All the judgments of Your mouth.
14 *I have rejoiced in the way of Your testimonies,*
   As much as in all riches.
15 *I will meditate on Your precepts,*
   And contemplate Your ways.
16 *I will delight myself in Your statutes;*
   I will not forget Your word.
17 *Deal bountifully with Your servant,*
   That I may live and keep Your word.
18 *Open my eyes, that I may see*
   Wondrous things from Your law.
19 *I am a stranger in the earth;*
   Do not hide Your commandments from me.
20 *My soul breaks with longing*
   For Your judgments at all times.
21 *You rebuke the proud—the cursed,*
   Who stray from Your commandments.
22 *Remove from me reproach and contempt,*
   For I have kept Your testimonies.
23 *Princes also sit and speak against me,*
   But Your servant meditates on Your statutes.
24 *Your testimonies also are my delight*
   And my counselors.
25 *My soul clings to the dust;*
   Revive me according to Your word.
26 *I have declared my ways, and You answered me;*
   Teach me Your statutes.
27 *Make me understand the way of Your precepts;*
   So shall I meditate on Your wondrous works.
28 *My soul melts from heaviness;*
   Strengthen me according to Your word.
29 *Remove from me the way of lying,*
   And grant me Your law graciously.
30 *I have chosen the way of truth;*
   Your judgments I have laid before me.
31 *I cling to Your testimonies;*
   O Lord, do not put me to shame!
32 *I will run the course of Your commandments,*
   For You shall enlarge my heart.
33 *Teach me, O Lord, the way of Your statutes,*
   And I shall keep it to the end.
34 *Give me understanding, and I shall keep Your law;*

Indeed, I shall observe it with my whole heart.
35 *Make me walk in the path of Your commandments,*
   For I delight in it.
36 *Incline my heart to Your testimonies,*
   And not to covetousness.
37 *Turn away my eyes from looking at worthless things,*
   And revive me in Your way.
38 *Establish Your word to Your servant,*
   Who is devoted to fearing You.
39 *Turn away my reproach which I dread,*
   For Your judgments are good.
40 *Behold, I long for Your precepts;*
   Revive me in Your righteousness.
41 *Let Your mercies come also to me, O Lord—*
   Your salvation according to Your word.
42 *So shall I have an answer for him who reproaches me,*
   For I trust in Your word.
43 *And take not the word of truth utterly out of my mouth,*
   For I have hoped in Your ordinances.
44 *So shall I keep Your law continually,*
   Forever and ever.
45 *And I will walk at liberty,*
   For I seek Your precepts.
46 *I will speak of Your testimonies also before kings,*
   And will not be ashamed.
47 *And I will delight myself in Your commandments,*
   Which I love.
48 *My hands also I will lift up to Your commandments,*
   Which I love,
   And I will meditate on Your statutes.

Exploring the Meaning

8) How does the psalmist's response to God's Word compare with the response of the people to God's Word in Nehemiah 8?

_____

_____

_____

9) Read Ezra 7:10. How was Ezra uniquely qualified to expound God's Word to God's people?

_____

_____

_____

10) Read Jeremiah 15:16. What is the connection between God's Word and joy?

_____

_____

_____

(verses to consider: Psalm 1:2; 19:8; 112:1; 119:111)

Summing Up...

"The Bible is . . . a source of happiness. Speaking of God's wisdom, the writer of Proverbs said, 'Blessed [or happy] is the man who listens to me' (Prov. 8:34). Jesus said, 'Blessed are those who hear the word of God, and observe it' (Luke 11:28). No person can be happier than when he discovers, accepts, and obeys God's Word."—*John MacArthur*

Reflecting on the Text

11) If you were not a Christian and you continually met believers who had never read the entire Bible and were largely ignorant of its content, what would you think of them? What would you think of Christianity in general?

_____

_____

_____

12) Is your heart and soul glad as you gather with other believers to hear God's Word preached or taught? If not, why? What safeguards can you put in

place to guard against apathy toward God's Word? What can you personally do to experience a greater joy in hearing and doing what the Scriptures say?

_____

_____

_____

13) How can you emulate the response of the Israelites (in Nehemiah 8) in your own life? Put another way, what specific changes in your relationship to the Word of God do you feel the need to change this week? How will you implement those changes?

_____

_____

_____

14) Based on this passage, what would you say to the Christian who claimed, "I don't need to gather with other believers; I can worship God and read His Word on my own"?

_____

_____

_____

Recording Your Thoughts

_____

_____

_____

For further study, see the following passages:

Numbers 29:35	Deuteronomy 31:10–13	Deuteronomy 33:10
2 Chronicles 8:13	Psalm 119:49–176	Malachi 2:7
Matthew 13:1–9, 18–23	Luke 10:38–43	John 4:34
Romans 3:20	Galatians 3:24	1 Timothy 4:13
James 1:22–25		

Getting Right with God

Opening Thought

1) A friend comes to you after a long period of living to please self instead of God. As in the story of the prodigal son (Luke 15), he/she expresses a desire to turn from such a sinful life and "come home" to God? What is necessary for this person to get right with God?

_____

_____

2) Is forgiveness a condition, a feeling, or both?

_____

_____

3) A growing number of voices today are arguing that worship has become, in many churches, very "creature-centered." In other words, the focus is not truly on God-—His greatness and worth—but rather on us—our needs and desires and what we can get from God. Do you agree with this critique? Why or why not? If this is an accurate portrayal, what is wrong with the status quo?

_____

_____

4) What is the most moving worship service you've ever experienced? What made it so powerful?

_____

_____

Background of the Passage

The focal point of Nehemiah 9 is not walls, not the enemies of God, not a great leader, not even the people of God. The focal point is God Himself. The public reading of the Word of God (Nehemiah 8) has pricked the hearts of the weary wall-builders. The result is that the listeners have been reminded of God's greatness and of their own failure to adequately live for His glory.

The long confession of sin that follows (vv. 4–37) occurs in the context of the recitation of God's mighty redemptive acts on Israel's behalf. This prayer of humility brings to mind many of the psalms in their theme and purpose. This season of national humiliation centers on adoring God for His great mercy in the forgiveness of their multiplied iniquities, in delivering them from judgment, protecting them, and blessing them graciously.

Apparently, this great prayer of worship offered to God was recited by a group of Levites (vv. 4, 5) indicating it had been prepared and adopted beforehand, probably by Ezra. This prayer initiated three hours of confession and worship (v. 3), which led to a national promise of obedience to God in the future (v. 38). The prayer itself is a quick lesson in Israelite history. It recounts God's mercy and power in the Exodus (vv. 9–12), during the months at Sinai (vv. 12–19), during the 38 years of wandering in the wilderness (vv. 19–21), during the period of possessing the Promised Land (vv. 22–25), and during the period from the judges to the Assyrian deportation (722 B.C.) and Babylonian exile (586 B.C.) (vv. 26–31).

Though well-intentioned, the people of God would ultimately fail to maintain this revival.

Bible Passage

Read 9:1–38, noting the key words and definitions to the right of the passage.

Nehemiah 9:1–38:

¹ *Now on the twenty-fourth day of this month the children of Israel were assembled with fasting, in sackcloth, and with dust on their heads.*

² *Then those of Israelite lineage separated themselves from all foreigners; and they stood and confessed their sins and the iniquities of their fathers.*

this month (v. 1)—Tishri (Sept./Oct.) 445 B.C. (see 7:73b; 8:2)

with fasting, in sackcloth, and with dust (v. 1)—The outward demonstration of deep mourning and heaviness of heart for their iniquity seems to have

³ *And they stood up in their place and read from the Book of the Law of the* LORD *their God for one-fourth of the day; and for another fourth they confessed and worshiped the* LORD *their God.*

⁴ *Then Jeshua, Bani, Kadmiel, Shebaniah, Bunni, Sherebiah, Bani, and Chenani stood on the stairs of the Levites and cried out with a loud voice to the* LORD *their God.*

⁵ *And the Levites, Jeshua, Kadmiel, Bani, Hashabniah, Sherebiah, Hodijah, Shebaniah, and Pethahiah, said:*

"Stand up and bless the LORD *your God Forever and ever!*

"Blessed be Your glorious name,
Which is exalted above all blessing and praise!

⁶ *You alone are the* LORD*;*
You have made heaven,
The heaven of heavens, with all their host,
The earth and everything on it,
The seas and all that is in them,
And You preserve them all.
The host of heaven worships You.

⁷ *"You are the* LORD *God,*
Who chose Abram,
And brought him out of Ur of the Chaldeans,
And gave him the name Abraham;

⁸ *You found his heart faithful before You,*
And made a covenant with him
To give the land of the Canaanites,
The Hittites, the Amorites,
the Perizzites, the Jebusites,
And the Girgashites—
To give it to his descendants.
You have performed Your words,
For You are righteous.

⁹ *"You saw the affliction of our fathers in Egypt,*
And heard their cry by the Red Sea.

¹⁰ *You showed signs and wonders against Pharaoh,*
Against all his servants,
And against all the people of his land.
For You knew that they acted proudly against them.

been done in the spirit of the Day of Atonement, which was normally observed on the tenth day of the seventh month.

separated themselves from all foreigners (v. 2)—This call for divorcing all lawful wives taken from among the heathen was needed, since the last time, prompted thirteen years before by Ezra, had been only partially successful. Many had escaped the required action of divorce and kept their pagan wives. Perhaps new defaulters had appeared also, and were confronted for the first time with this necessary action of divorce. Nehemiah's efforts were successful in removing this evil mixture.

they stood . . . read . . . confessed and worshiped (v. 3)—The succession of events helped to reestablish the essential commitment of Israel to God and His law. They read for three hours about the sins of their fathers and for three more hours confessed that they had been partakers of similar evil deeds. In response to all of this, they worshiped.

have made heaven (v. 6)—The recitation was ordered historically, although themes of promise and judgment are traced through Israel's history with God. The first feature is the celebration of God's greatness as Creator (see Gen. 1–2).

The host of heaven worships You (v. 6)—The praise which Israel offered on earth was also echoed in the heavens by angelic hosts.

found his heart faithful before You (v. 8)—The Abrahamic Covenant (Gen. 17:1–9) was based on God's faithfulness to His Word and given to a man who was faithful to Him.

So You made a name for Yourself, as it is this day.

11 *And You divided the sea before them,*
So that they went through the midst of the sea on the dry land;
And their persecutors You threw into the deep,
As a stone into the mighty waters.

12 *Moreover You led them by day with a cloudy pillar,*
And by night with a pillar of fire,
To give them light on the road
Which they should travel.

13 *"You came down also on Mount Sinai,*
And spoke with them from heaven,
And gave them just ordinances and true laws,
Good statutes and commandments.

14 *You made known to them Your holy Sabbath,*
And commanded them precepts, statutes and laws,
By the hand of Moses Your servant.

15 *You gave them bread from heaven for their hunger,*
And brought them water out of the rock for their thirst,
And told them to go in to possess the land
Which You had sworn to give them.

16 *"But they and our fathers acted proudly,*
Hardened their necks,
And did not heed Your commandments.

17 *They refused to obey,*
And they were not mindful of Your wonders
That You did among them.
But they hardened their necks,
And in their rebellion
They appointed a leader
To return to their bondage.
But You are God,
Ready to pardon,
Gracious and merciful,
Slow to anger,
Abundant in kindness,

a covenant with him to give the land (v. 8)—The covenant was a covenant of salvation, but also involved the Promised Land. The people, having just returned from captivity, understandably emphasized that feature of the covenant, since God had returned them to the Land.

made a name for Yourself (v. 10)—God established His righteous reputation over the powers of Egypt by the miracles of immense power performed in Egypt.

They appointed a leader (v. 17)—The Hebrew of this statement is almost a repeat of Numbers 14:4, which records the discontent of the people with God's plan and Moses's leadership.

And did not forsake them.

18 "Even when they made a molded calf for
themselves,
And said, 'This is your god
That brought you up out of Egypt,'
And worked great provocations,

19 Yet in Your manifold mercies
You did not forsake them in the wilderness.
The pillar of the cloud did not depart from them
by day,
To lead them on the road;
Nor the pillar of fire by night,
To show them light,
And the way they should go.

20 You also gave Your good Spirit to instruct them,
And did not withhold Your manna from their
mouth,
And gave them water for their thirst.

21 Forty years You sustained them in the wilderness,
They lacked nothing;
Their clothes did not wear out
And their feet did not swell.

22 "Moreover You gave them kingdoms and nations,
And divided them into districts.
So they took possession of the land of Sihon,
The land of the king of Heshbon,
And the land of Og king of Bashan.

23 You also multiplied their children as the stars
of heaven,
And brought them into the land
Which You had told their fathers
To go in and possess.

24 So the people went in
And possessed the land;
You subdued before them the inhabitants of
the land,
The Canaanites,
And gave them into their hands,
With their kings
And the people of the land,
That they might do with them as they wished.

They lacked nothing (v. 21)—
The same word is used in Ps.
23:1, "I shall not want." Even during the long season of chastisement, God miraculously cared for their every need.

gave them kingdoms and nations (v. 22)—Canaan was comprised of a number of politically semi-autonomous groups all loosely connected under the waning authority of Egypt. The Lord divided Canaan into tribal districts, thus apportioning the Land for Israel's possession.

multiplied their children (v. 23)—A nation of offspring was another aspect of the promise made to Abraham (Gen. 12:1–3). God told Abraham that his seed would be like the stars of heaven (Gen. 15:5), and Exodus 1:1–3 reminded Israel that their multiplication in Egypt was nothing short of miraculous.

subdued before them (v. 24) —Moses said in Exodus 15:3, "The LORD is a man of war." As Israel's military leader and king, He led them into battle to defeat their enemies and take the Land.

25 *And they took strong cities and a rich land,*
   And possessed houses full of all goods,
   Cisterns already dug, vineyards, olive groves,
   And fruit trees in abundance.
   So they ate and were filled and grew fat,
   And delighted themselves in Your great goodness.
26 *"Nevertheless they were disobedient*
   And rebelled against You,
   Cast Your law behind their backs
   And killed Your prophets, who testified against
   them
   To turn them to Yourself;
   And they worked great provocations.
27 *Therefore You delivered them into the hand of*
   their enemies,
   Who oppressed them;
   And in the time of their trouble,
   When they cried to You,
   You heard from heaven;
   And according to Your abundant mercies
   You gave them deliverers who saved them
   From the hand of their enemies.
28 *"But after they had rest,*
   They again did evil before You.
   Therefore You left them in the hand of their
   enemies,
   So that they had dominion over them;
   Yet when they returned and cried out to You,
   You heard from heaven;
   And many times You delivered them according to
   Your mercies,
29 *And testified against them,*
   That You might bring them back to Your law.
   Yet they acted proudly,
   And did not heed Your commandments,
   But sinned against Your judgments,
   'Which if a man does, he shall live by them.'
   And they shrugged their shoulders,
   Stiffened their necks,
   And would not hear.
30 *Yet for many years You had patience with them,*

who testified against them
(v. 26—God's prophets brought them to God's court to be judged by His law. This theme is repeated throughout the message (vv. 29, 30, 34).

And testified against them by Your Spirit in Your prophets.
Yet they would not listen;
Therefore You gave them into the hand of the peoples of the lands.
31 Nevertheless in Your great mercy
You did not utterly consume them nor forsake them;
For You are God, gracious and merciful.
32 "Now therefore, our God,
The great, the mighty, and awesome God,
Who keeps covenant and mercy:
Do not let all the trouble seem small before You
That has come upon us,
Our kings and our princes,
Our priests and our prophets,
Our fathers and on all Your people, from the days of the kings of Assyria until this day.
33 However You are just in all that has befallen us;
For You have dealt faithfully,
But we have done wickedly.
34 Neither our kings nor our princes,
Our priests nor our fathers,
Have kept Your law,
Nor heeded Your commandments and Your testimonies,
With which You testified against them.
35 For they have not served You in their kingdom,
Or in the many good things that You gave them,
Or in the large and rich land which You set before them;
Nor did they turn from their wicked works.
36 "Here we are, servants today!
And the land that You gave to our fathers,
To eat its fruit and its bounty,
Here we are, servants in it!
37 And it yields much increase to the kings
You have set over us,
Because of our sins;
Also they have dominion over our bodies and our cattle

Now therefore (v. 32)—Having reviewed the faithfulness of God to the Abrahamic Covenant (vv. 7–8) throughout Israel's national history, the prayer picks up with the present time, confessing their unfaithfulness to (vv. 33–35) and renewed commitment to the Mosaic Covenant (vv. 36–38).

kings of Assyria . . . this day (v. 32)—This statement sweeps across a summary of Assyrian, Babylonian, and Persian domination of the nation for almost four centuries up to that time.

in it . . . over us (vv. 36–37)—The praise prayer rejoices that the Jews have been returned to the Land, but grieves that Gentiles still rule over them.

much increase to the kings (v. 37)—Because God's people continued in widespread sin, enemy kings enjoyed the bounty that would have been Israel's.

At their pleasure;
And we are in great distress.
38 *"And because of all this,*
We make a sure covenant, and write it; our
leaders, our Levites, and our priests seal it."

because of all this (v. 38)— The history of God's faithfulness, in spite of Israel's unfaithfulness, is the ground of a pledge and promise which the people make to obey God and not repeat the sins of their fathers.

We make a sure covenant and write it (v. 38)—A covenant was a binding agreement between two parties. In short, it was a formalized relationship with commitments to loyalty. In this case, the nation initiated this covenant with God.

Understanding the Text

5) How did the people of God demonstrate their spirit of repentance in this chapter?

_____

_____

_____

_____

(verses to consider: 2 Chronicles 7:14; Ezra 9:1–15)

6) What role did the Levites play in this solemn assembly?

_____

_____

_____

_____

7) What does this prayer reveal about the character and nature of God, and why is this important in all our praying?

_____

_____

_____

_____

_____

(verses to consider: Leviticus 20:26; Psalm 145:1–6; Philippians 2:9–11; 1 Peter 1:15)

8) What does this prayer say specifically about human stubbornness and pride?

_____

_____

_____

_____

_____

Cross Reference

Read Exodus 24:1–8.

¹ Now He said to Moses, "Come up to the LORD, you and Aaron, Nadab and Abihu, and seventy of the elders of Israel, and worship from afar.

² "And Moses alone shall come near the LORD, but they shall not come near; nor shall the people go up with him."

³ So Moses came and told the people all the words of the LORD and all the judgments. And all the people answered with one voice and said, "All the words which the LORD has said we will do."

⁴ And Moses wrote all the words of the LORD. And he rose early in the morning, and built an altar at the foot of the mountain, and twelve pillars according to the twelve tribes of Israel.

⁵ Then he sent young men of the children of Israel, who offered burnt offerings and sacrificed peace offerings of oxen to the LORD.

⁶ And Moses took half the blood and put it in basins, and half the blood he sprinkled on the altar.

⁷ Then he took the Book of the Covenant and read in the hearing of the people. And they said, "All that the LORD has said we will do, and be obedient."

⁸ And Moses took the blood, sprinkled it on the people, and said, "This is the blood of the covenant which the LORD has made with you according to all these words."

Exploring the Meaning

9) How does the situation in Exodus 24 compare and contrast with the situation the people of God faced in Nehemiah 9?

_____

_____

_____

_____

_____

10) Read Psalm 78. What does this "song" teach you about human pride and foolishness?

_____

_____

_____

_____

_____

11) Read 1 John 1:5–10. What does this New Testament passage teach believers about confessing sin?

_____

_____

_____

_____

_____

Summing Up...

"The church today is often guilty of supplying believers with the paper armor of good advice, programs, activities, techniques, and methods—when what they need is the godly armor of holy living. No program, method, or technique can bring wholeness and happiness to the believer who is unwilling to confront and forsake his sin."—*John MacArthur*

Reflecting on the Text

12) What lessons from the past do you need to remember today to keep you from making foolish choices with devastating consequences?

_____

_____

_____

_____

_____

13) If you were to write your own spiritual history, how would it compare to Israel's experience? How would it be different?

_____

_____

_____

_____

_____

14) What are some specific ways God has revealed His love and mercy to you?

_____

_____

_____

_____

_____

15) In what ways are your prayers man-centered? God-centered?

_____

_____

_____

_____

_____

16) What is the right response when we become aware of overt sin or subtle rebelliousness in our lives?

_____

_____

_____

_____

_____

Recording Your Thoughts

_____

_____

_____

_____

_____

_____

For further study, see the following passages:

Genesis 12:1–3	Genesis 15:4–7	Exodus 1:1–3
Exodus 15:3	Leviticus 16:1–34	Leviticus 23:26–32
Numbers 14:4	Deuteronomy 6:4–6	Ezra 10
Psalm 23:1	Psalm 115	Isaiah 40
Matthew 10:29	Romans 1:25	Romans 4
1 John 3:1–3		

Making a Fresh Start

Opening Thought

1) Do you ever make New Year's resolutions? Why or why not? If you do make them, how effectively do you keep them?

_____

_____

_____

_____

2) Some churches require new members to sign a "covenant statement" or "membership agreement" in which the signer pledges to fulfill certain obligations. Is this a good idea? Is it necessary? Why or why not?

_____

_____

_____

_____

_____

3) When are written contracts a wise course of action?

_____

_____

_____

_____

_____

Background of the Passage

History is replete with Christians who tearfully admitted their sins only to leave the church gathering and immediately resume a life of carnality. It is one thing to express regret and words of sorrow; it is another to follow up prayers of confession with deeds of repentance.

In the Old Testament Book of Nehemiah, after the Jewish people completed a great construction project (that is, rebuilding the walls of Jerusalem), they commenced a great consecration project (that is, recommitting themselves to the Lord). Ezra's teaching of the Law of God (ch. 8) resulted in a genuine confession of sin (ch. 9). Then, to demonstrate their sincere resolve to change, the Israelites made a covenant with God.

The 84 sealed signatures on the covenant are a list of Israel's leaders-priests, Levites, and other officials (10:1–27). Surprisingly, Ezra's name is not listed. Primarily they were pledging to submit to the Word of God and to separate themselves from their pagan, Gentile neighbors. But the covenant also included matters involving the temple (vv. 32–39). Laws for all the offerings and titles were reinstated so as not to "neglect the house of our God" (v. 39).

Bible Passage

Read 10:1–39, noting the key words and definitions to the right of the passage.

Nehemiah 10:1–39:
¹ *Now those who placed their seal on the document were: Nehemiah the governor, the son of Hacaliah, and Zedekiah,*
² *Seraiah, Azariah, Jeremiah,*
³ *Pashhur, Amariah, Malchijah,*
⁴ *Hattush, Shebaniah, Malluch,*
⁵ *Harim, Meremoth, Obadiah,*
⁶ *Daniel, Ginnethon, Baruch,*
⁷ *Meshullam, Abijah, Mijamin,*
⁸ *Maaziah, Bilgai, and Shemaiah. These were the priests.*
⁹ *The Levites: Jeshua the son of Azaniah, Binnui of the sons of Henadad, and Kadmiel.*
¹⁰ *Their brethren: Shebaniah, Hodijah, Kelita,*

Pelaiah, Hanan,

¹¹ *Micha, Rehob, Hashabiah,*

¹² *Zaccur, Sherebiah, Shebaniah,*

¹³ *Hodijah, Bani, and Beninu.*

¹⁴ *The leaders of the people: Parosh, Pahath-Moab, Elam, Zattu, Bani,*

¹⁵ *Bunni, Azgad, Bebai,*

¹⁶ *Adonijah, Bigvai, Adin,*

¹⁷ *Ater, Hezekiah, Azzur,*

¹⁸ *Hodijah, Hashum, Bezai,*

¹⁹ *Hariph, Anathoth, Nebai,*

²⁰ *Magpiash, Meshullam, Hezir,*

²¹ *Meshezabel, Zadok, Jaddua,*

²² *Pelatiah, Hanan, Anaiah,*

²³ *Hoshea, Hananiah, Hasshub,*

²⁴ *Hallohesh, Pilha, Shobek,*

²⁵ *Rehum, Hashabnah, Maaseiah,*

²⁶ *Ahijah, Hanan, Anan,*

²⁷ *Malluch, Harim, and Baanah.*

²⁸ *Now the rest of the people-the priests, the Levites, the gatekeepers, the singers, the Nethinim, and all those who had separated themselves from the peoples of the lands to the Law of God, their wives, their sons, and their daughters, everyone who had knowledge and understanding—*

²⁹ *these joined with their brethren, their nobles, and entered into a curse and an oath to walk in God's Law, which was given by Moses the servant of God, and to observe and do all the commandments of the L*LOR* our Lord, and His ordinances and His statutes:*

³⁰ *We would not give our daughters as wives to the peoples of the land, nor take their daughters for our sons;*

³¹ *if the peoples of the land brought wares or any grain to sell on the Sabbath day, we would not buy it from them on the Sabbath, or on a holy day; and we would forego the seventh year's produce and the exacting of every debt.*

³² *Also we made ordinances for ourselves, to exact from ourselves yearly one-third of a shekel for the service of the house of our God:*

Nethinim (v. 28)—see Ezra 2:43–54

who had separated themselves (v. 28)—These are those who (1) had followed the demand of Ezra and Nehemiah to divorce pagan spouses or (2) had been left in the Land but never joined themselves to any heathen, thus remaining separate. Intermarriage with the nations had previously precipitated an influence in Israel which had culminated in Babylonian slavery, thus playing a major role in Israel's unfaithfulness to the covenant.

a curse and an oath (v. 29)—Covenants characteristically were ratified by an oath ceremony in which the parties swore to the terms of the covenant. A curse rite was often included wherein the slaughtering of an animal indicated similar consequences for the covenant breaker. Israel's pledged adherence to the law was thus solemnly affirmed.

not give our daughters . . . nor take their daughters (v. 30)—Parents controlled marriages, so this part of the covenant came from them. Again, it stressed the serious matter of marrying a heathen from an idolatrous people (see Ezra 10).

we made ordinances (vv. 32–33)—What the people were committing themselves to do by covenant turned into law requiring a one-third shekel temple tax. The Mosaic ordinance required one-half of a shekel, but the severe economic straits of the time led to the reduced amount. By the time of Christ, the people had returned to the Mosaic stipulation of one-half of a shekel.

33 *for the showbread, for the regular grain offering, for the regular burnt offering of the Sabbaths, the New Moons, and the set feasts; for the holy things, for the sin offerings to make atonement for Israel, and all the work of the house of our God.*

34 *We cast lots among the priests, the Levites, and the people, for bringing the wood offering into the house of our God, according to our fathers' houses, at the appointed times year by year, to burn on the altar of the LORD our God as it is written in the Law.*

35 *And we made ordinances to bring the firstfruits of our ground and the firstfruits of all fruit of all trees, year by year, to the house of the LORD;*

36 *to bring the firstborn of our sons and our cattle, as it is written in the Law, and the firstborn of our herds and our flocks, to the house of our God, to the priests who minister in the house of our God;*

37 *to bring the firstfruits of our dough, our offerings, the fruit from all kinds of trees, the new wine and oil, to the priests, to the storerooms of the house of our God; and to bring the tithes of our land to the Levites, for the Levites should receive the tithes in all our farming communities.*

38 *And the priest, the descendant of Aaron, shall be with the Levites when the Levites receive tithes; and the Levites shall bring up a tenth of the tithes to the house of our God, to the rooms of the storehouse.*

39 *For the children of Israel and the children of Levi shall bring the offering of the grain, of the new wine and the oil, to the storerooms where the articles of the sanctuary are, where the priests who minister and the gatekeepers and the singers are; and we will not neglect the house of our God.*

for bringing the wood offering into the house of our God (v. 34)—The carrying of the wood for the constantly burning altar had formerly been the duty of the Nethinim, but few of them had returned from Babylon (7:60) so more people were chosen to assist in this task.

firstfruits . . . firstborn . . . firstborn (vv. 35–37)—These laws required the firstfruits of the ground, the firstfruits of the trees, the firstborn sons redeemed by the estimated price of the priest, and the firstborn of the herds and flocks. All of this was kept at the storehouses near the temple and distributed for the support of the priests and Levites. The Levites then gave a tenth of what they received to the priests.

Understanding the Text

4) What circumstances motivated the Israelites to make and sign a written agreement?

_____

_____

_____

5) What specific promises or pledges did the agreement between the Israelites and God contain? Why were such vows or oaths viewed so seriously?

_____

_____

_____

(verses to consider: Ecclesiastes 5:1–7; Matthew 5:33–37; 23:16–22)

6) What provisions did the oath between Israel and God include for the provision and upkeep of the priests and the temple?

_____

_____

_____

_____

7) Why was there such an emphasis on "first" things?

_____

_____

_____

_____

(verses to consider: Exodus 13:12; 23:19; 34:26; Numbers 18:13–17; Deuteronomy 26:2)

Cross Reference

Read Deuteronomy 29:1–13.

1 *These are the words of the covenant which the LORD commanded Moses to make with the children of Israel in the land of Moab, besides the covenant which He made with them in Horeb.*

2 *Now Moses called all Israel and said to them: "You have seen all that the LORD did before your eyes in the land of Egypt, to Pharaoh and to all his servants and to all his land—*

3 *"the great trials which your eyes have seen, the signs, and those great wonders.*

4 *"Yet the LORD has not given you a heart to perceive and eyes to see and ears to hear, to this very day.*

5 *"And I have led you forty years in the wilderness. Your clothes have not worn out on you, and your sandals have not worn out on your feet.*

6 *"You have not eaten bread, nor have you drunk wine or similar drink, that you may know that I am the LORD your God.*

7 *And when you came to this place, Sihon king of Heshbon and Og king of Bashan came out against us to battle, and we conquered them.*

8 *"We took their land and gave it as an inheritance to the Reubenites, to the Gadites, and to half the tribe of Manasseh.*

9 *"Therefore keep the words of this covenant, and do them, that you may prosper in all that you do.*

10 *"All of you stand today before the LORD your God: your leaders and your tribes and your elders and your officers, all the men of Israel,*

11 *"your little ones and your wives—also the stranger who is in your camp, from the one who cuts your wood to the one who draws your water—*

12 *"that you may enter into covenant with the LORD your God, and into His oath, which the Lord your God makes with you today,*

13 *"that He may establish you today as a people for Himself, and that He may be God to you, just as He has spoken to you, and just as He has sworn to your fathers, to Abraham, Isaac, and Jacob.*

Exploring the Meaning

8) Why might this have been the passage that the Israelites used in recommitting themselves to God?

_____

_____

_____

_____

9) Read Exodus 34:10–17. How are "mixed marriages" spiritually dangerous?

_____

_____

_____

(verses to consider: Malachi 2:10–12; 1 Corinthians 7:39; 2 Corinthians 6:14–7:1)

10) Read Matthew 6:19–21. How does our stewardship of money and possessions reveal our true priorities?

_____

_____

_____

Summing Up...

"Every true Christian has in his heart a sense of the moral excellence of God's Law. And the more mature he becomes in Christ, the more fully he perceives and lauds the law's goodness, holiness, and glory. The more profoundly he is committed to the direction of the Holy Spirit in his life, the deeper his love for the Lord Jesus Christ becomes, the deeper his sense of God's holiness and majesty becomes, and the greater will be his longing to fulfill God's law."
—John MacArthur

Reflecting on the Text

11) When in your life have difficult circumstances motivated you to recommit yourself to the Lord? Do you need to do so now? If so, in what specific areas?

_____

_____

_____

12) Is it helpful to you to write out your spiritual commitments and intentions? Why or why not?

_____

_____

_____

13) Who can help hold you accountable in your quest for a deeper, richer, more consistent walk?

_____

_____

_____

Recording Your Thoughts

_____

_____

_____

_____

_____

_____

_____

For further study, see the following passages:

Exodus 30:11–16	Exodus 34:19–20	Exodus 35:1–3
Leviticus 6:12–13	Leviticus 27:30–34	Numbers 28:25–32
Deuteronomy 26:1–11	Isaiah 60:1–2	Matthew 17:24–27
Luke 2:22–24	Acts 7:48–50	

Rededicating the Wall

Opening Thought

1) If you could visit any city in the world, which one would you choose and why? If you were required to move to and live in a major world city, which would it be and why?

_____

_____

_____

_____

2) What are the pros and cons of living in the country? Of living in the city?

_____

_____

_____

_____

3) In many churches today, believers engage in "worship wars" (conflicts over music or liturgy). Is this phenomenon just a matter of personal preference, or is it an issue of biblical truth?

_____

_____

_____

_____

_____

Background of the Passage

Christianity is, at its heart, all about sacrifice. Christ gave His life on the cross as a full and final payment for the sins of the world. The elect put their faith in Christ alone and then embark on a life of sacrifice. They give themselves fully and completely to His service. The result is that God is glorified, and the people of God are satisfied.

In chapters 11 and 12 of Nehemiah we find the details of Nehemiah's exercising his governorship. He understood that a rebuilt city requires an energized and committed populace. Consequently, lots were cast to determine who would inhabit the holy city. An adequate number of temple workers were needed. Nehemiah also made provisions for an adequate number of worshipers.

There followed a marvelous dedicatory service, during which the people kept their promises to support the work of the temple through tithes and offerings. The mood on this occasion was one of pure joy, thus proving that God's glory and man's deep happiness are not at odds. Rather, they fit together, like hand in glove.

Study these chapters carefully for a wonderful reminder of the blessings of sacrificial living.

Bible Passage

Read 11:1—12:47, noting the key words and definitions to the right of the passage.

Nehemiah 11:1—12:47:

¹ Now the leaders of the people dwelt at Jerusalem; the rest of the people cast lots to bring one out of ten to dwell in Jerusalem, the holy city, and nine-tenths were to dwell in other cities.

² And the people blessed all the men who willingly offered themselves to dwell at Jerusalem.

³ These are the heads of the province who dwelt in Jerusalem. (But in the cities of Judah everyone dwelt in his own possession in their

cast lots (v. 1)—A method of decision making which God honored. Nehemiah redistributed the population so that one out of every ten Jews lived in Jerusalem. The other nine were free to reestablish their family heritage in the Land.

These are the heads of the province (vv. 3–24)—The people who dwelt in Jerusalem are identified.

cities—Israelites, priests, Levites, Nethinim, and descendants of Solomon's servants.)

4 Also in Jerusalem dwelt some of the children of Judah and of the children of Benjamin.
The children of Judah: Athaiah the son of Uzziah, the son of Zechariah, the son of Amariah, the son of Shephatiah, the son of Mahalalel, of the children of Perez;

5 and Maaseiah the son of Baruch, the son of Col-Hozeh, the son of Hazaiah, the son of Adaiah, the son of Joiarib, the son of Zechariah, the son of Shiloni.

6 All the sons of Perez who dwelt at Jerusalem were four hundred and sixty-eight valiant men.

7 And these are the sons of Benjamin: Sallu the son of Meshullam, the son of Joed, the son of Pedaiah, the son of Kolaiah, the son of Maaseiah, the son of Ithiel, the son of Jeshaiah;

8 and after him Gabbai and Sallai, nine hundred and twenty-eight.

9 Joel the son of Zichri was their overseer, and Judah the son of Senuah was second over the city.

10 Of the priests: Jedaiah the son of Joiarib, and Jachin;

11 Seraiah the son of Hilkiah, the son of Meshullam, the son of Zadok, the son of Meraioth, the son of Ahitub, was the leader of the house of God.

12 Their brethren who did the work of the house were eight hundred and twenty-two; and Adaiah the son of Jeroham, the son of Pelaliah, the son of Amzi, the son of Zechariah, the son of Pashhur, the son of Malchijah,

13 and his brethren, heads of the fathers' houses, were two hundred and forty-two; and Amashai the son of Azarel, the son of Ahzai, the son of Meshillemoth, the son of Immer,

14 and their brethren, mighty men of valor, were one hundred and twenty-eight. Their overseer was Zabdiel the son of one of the great men.

15 Also of the Levites: Shemaiah the son of Hasshub, the son of Azrikam, the son of Hashabiah, the son of Bunni;

16 Shabbethai and Jozabad, of the heads of the

Ophel (v. 21)—see note on 3:26

And as for the villages (vv. 25–36)—These are the places where 90 percent of the people dwelt outside of Jerusalem (see Ezra 2:21–23, 27, 34).

Zerubbabel (12:1)–see Ezra 2:2

Jeshua (12:1)—see Ezra 2:2

Jeshua begot Joiakim (vv. 10–11)—This record lists six generations of high priests, beginning with Jeshua. The Jonathan of verse 11 is the Johanan of verse 22.

the heads of the fathers' houses were (vv. 12–21)—Each of the 22 families in verses 1–7 is repeated, except one (see Hattush, verse 2). Perhaps by the time of Joiakim's high priesthood, this family had become extinct, the fathers having no male offspring.

Levites, had the oversight of the business outside of the house of God;

¹⁷ *Mattaniah the son of Micha, the son of Zabdi, the son of Asaph, the leader who began the thanksgiving with prayer; Bakbukiah, the second among his brethren; and Abda the son of Shammua, the son of Galal, the son of Jeduthun.*

¹⁸ *All the Levites in the holy city were two hundred and eighty-four.*

¹⁹ *Moreover the gatekeepers, Akkub, Talmon, and their brethren who kept the gates, were one hundred and seventy-two.*

²⁰ *And the rest of Israel, of the priests and Levites, were in all the cities of Judah, everyone in his inheritance.*

²¹ *But the Nethinim dwelt in Ophel. And Ziha and Gishpa were over the Nethinim.*

²² *Also the overseer of the Levites at Jerusalem was Uzzi the son of Bani, the son of Hashabiah, the son of Mattaniah, the son of Micha, of the sons of Asaph, the singers in charge of the service of the house of God.*

²³ *For it was the king's command concerning them that a certain portion should be for the singers, a quota day by day.*

²⁴ *Pethahiah the son of Meshezabel, of the children of Zerah the son of Judah, was the king's deputy in all matters concerning the people.*

²⁵ *And as for the villages with their fields, some of the children of Judah dwelt in Kirjath Arba and its villages, Dibon and its villages, Jekabzeel and its villages;*

²⁶ *in Jeshua, Moladah, Beth Pelet,*

²⁷ *Hazar Shual, and Beersheba and its villages;*

²⁸ *in Ziklag and Meconah and its villages;*

²⁹ *in En Rimmon, Zorah, Jarmuth,*

³⁰ *Zanoah, Adullam, and their villages; in Lachish and its fields; in Azekah and its villages. They dwelt from Beersheba to the Valley of Hinnom.*

³¹ *Also the children of Benjamin from Geba dwelt in Michmash, Aija, and Bethel, and their villages;*

³² *in Anathoth, Nob, Ananiah;*

³³ *in Hazor, Ramah, Gittaim;*

³⁴ in Hadid, Zeboim, Neballat;

³⁵ in Lod, Ono, and the Valley of Craftsmen.

³⁶ Some of the Judean divisions of Levites were in Benjamin.

¹ Now these are the priests and the Levites who came up with Zerubbabel the son of Shealtiel, and Jeshua: Seraiah, Jeremiah, Ezra,

² Amariah, Malluch, Hattush,

³ Shechaniah, Rehum, Meremoth,

⁴ Iddo, Ginnethoi, Abijah,

⁵ Mijamin, Maadiah, Bilgah,

⁶ Shemaiah, Joiarib, Jedaiah,

⁷ Sallu, Amok, Hilkiah, and Jedaiah. These were the heads of the priests and their brethren in the days of Jeshua.

⁸ Moreover the Levites were Jeshua, Binnui, Kadmiel, Sherebiah, Judah, and Mattaniah who led the thanksgiving psalms, he and his brethren.

⁹ Also Bakbukiah and Unni, their brethren, stood across from them in their duties.

¹⁰ Jeshua begot Joiakim, Joiakim begot Eliashib, Eliashib begot Joiada,

¹¹ Joiada begot Jonathan, and Jonathan begot Jaddua.

¹² Now in the days of Joiakim, the priests, the heads of the fathers' houses were: of Seraiah, Meraiah; of Jeremiah, Hananiah;

¹³ of Ezra, Meshullam; of Amariah, Jehohanan;

¹⁴ of Melichu, Jonathan; of Shebaniah, Joseph;

¹⁵ of Harim, Adna; of Meraioth, Helkai;

¹⁶ of Iddo, Zechariah; of Ginnethon, Meshullam;

¹⁷ of Abijah, Zichri; the son of Minjamin; of Moadiah, Piltai;

¹⁸ of Bilgah, Shammua; of Shemaiah, Jehonathan;

¹⁹ of Joiarib, Mattenai; of Jedaiah, Uzzi;

²⁰ of Sallai, Kallai; of Amok, Eber;

²¹ of Hilkiah, Hashabiah; and of Jedaiah, Nethanel.

²² During the reign of Darius the Persian, a record was also kept of the Levites and priests who had been heads of their fathers' houses in the days of Eliashib, Joiada, Johanan, and Jaddua.

²³ The sons of Levi, the heads of the fathers' houses

Darius the Persian (v. 22)
—This refers to Darius II, who reigned about 423–404 B.C.

book of the chronicles (v. 23)
—literally "were written on the scroll of the matters of the days";

until the days of Johanan the son of Eliashib, were written in the book of the chronicles.

24 And the heads of the Levites were Hashabiah, Sherebiah, and Jeshua the son of Kadmiel, with their brothers across from them, to praise and give thanks, group alternating with group, according to the command of David the man of God.

25 Mattaniah, Bakbukiah, Obadiah, Meshullam, Talmon, and Akkub were gatekeepers keeping the watch at the storerooms of the gates.

26 These lived in the days of Joiakim the son of Jeshua, the son of Jozadak, and in the days of Nehemiah the governor, and of Ezra the priest, the scribe.

27 Now at the dedication of the wall of Jerusalem they sought out the Levites in all their places, to bring them to Jerusalem to celebrate the dedication with gladness, both with thanksgivings and singing, with cymbals and stringed instruments and harps.

28 And the sons of the singers gathered together from the countryside around Jerusalem, from the villages of the Netophathites,

29 from the house of Gilgal, and from the fields of Geba and Azmaveth; for the singers had built themselves villages all around Jerusalem.

30 Then the priests and Levites purified themselves, and purified the people, the gates, and the wall.

31 So I brought the leaders of Judah up on the wall, and appointed two large thanksgiving choirs. One went to the right hand on the wall toward the Refuse Gate.

32 After them went Hoshaiah and half of the leaders of Judah,

33 and Azariah, Ezra, Meshullam,

34 Judah, Benjamin, Shemaiah, Jeremiah,

35 and some of the priests' sons with trumpets—Zechariah the son of Jonathan, the son of Shemaiah, the son of Mattaniah, the son of Michaiah, the son of Zaccur, the son of Asaph,

36 and his brethren, Shemaiah, Azarel, Milalai, Gilalai, Maai, Nethanel, Judah, and Hanani, with the musical instruments of David the man

this involved precise genealogical records kept in the administrative archives of Judah

the dedication of the wall (vv. 27–43)—In the same manner marking the dedications of the temple in Solomon's day (2 Chr. 5–7) and the rebuilt temple several decades earlier (Ezra 6:16–18), the rebuilt walls were dedicated with the music of thanksgiving (most likely shortly after the events of Neh. 9).

purified (v. 30)—See Leviticus 16:30 for the sense of moral purity in this symbolic act.

So I brought the leaders of Judah up on the wall (vv. 31–40)—They probably assembled at the Valley Gate on the west. One of the choirs was led by Ezra (v. 36), the other accompanied by Nehemiah (v. 38). Moving in different directions (v. 38), they assembled together in the temple area (v. 40).

Refuse Gate (v. 31)—see notes on 2:13; 3:13

the musical instruments of David (v. 36)—This phrase could refer to the same kind of instruments David's musicians used or the actual instruments constructed in David's time, now being used centuries later (see 1 Chronicles 15:16).

the man of God (v. 36)—see Deuteronomy 33:1

of God. Ezra the scribe went before them.

37 By the Fountain Gate, in front of them, they went up the stairs of the City of David, on the stairway of the wall, beyond the house of David, as far as the Water Gate eastward.

38 The other thanksgiving choir went the opposite way, and I was behind them with half of the people on the wall, going past the Tower of the Ovens as far as the Broad Wall,

39 and above the Gate of Ephraim, above the Old Gate, above the Fish Gate, the Tower of Hananel, the Tower of the Hundred, as far as the Sheep Gate; and they stopped by the Gate of the Prison.

40 So the two thanksgiving choirs stood in the house of God, likewise I and the half of the rulers with me;

41 and the priests, Eliakim, Maaseiah, Minjamin, Michaiah, Elioenai, Zechariah, and Hananiah, with trumpets;

42 also Maaseiah, Shemaiah, Eleazar, Uzzi, Jehohanan, Malchijah, Elam, and Ezer. The singers sang loudly with Jezrahiah the director.

43 Also that day they offered great sacrifices, and rejoiced, for God had made them rejoice with great joy; the women and the children also rejoiced, so that the joy of Jerusalem was heard afar off.

44 And at the same time some were appointed over the rooms of the storehouse for the offerings, the firstfruits, and the tithes, to gather into them from the fields of the cities the portions specified by the Law for the priests and Levites; for Judah rejoiced over the priests and Levites who ministered.

45 Both the singers and the gatekeepers kept the charge of their God and the charge of the purification, according to the command of David and Solomon his son.

46 For in the days of David and Asaph of old there were chiefs of the singers, and songs of praise and thanksgiving to God.

47 In the days of Zerubbabel and in the days of Nehemiah all Israel gave the portions for the

the Fountain Gate (v. 37)—see note on 2:14

the Water Gate (v. 37)—see notes on 3:26; 8:16

opposite way (v. 38)—This second choir marched clockwise to the north (see 12:31).

Tower of the Ovens (v. 38)—see note on 3:11

the Gate of Ephraim (v. 39)—see note on 8:16

the Old Gate (v. 39)—see note on 3:6

the Fish Gate (v. 39)—see note on 3:3

the Tower of Hananel (v. 39)—see note on 3:1

the Tower of the Hundred (v. 39)—see note on 3:1

the Sheep Gate (v. 39)—see notes on 3:1, 32

the Gate of the Prison (v. 39)—located in the northeast section of Jerusalem

for God had made them rejoice (v. 43)—The God of all joy activated their inner joy, which brought corporate celebration. Though these may have been few and far between, moments like this characterized the life of obedience and blessing which God had set before Israel.

specified by the Law (v. 44)—see Leviticus 7:34–36

the command of David . . . Solomon (v. 45)—see 1 Chronicles 25–26

the children of Aaron (v. 47)—the priests

singers and the gatekeepers, a portion for each
day. They also consecrated holy things for the
Levites, and the Levites consecrated them for the
children of Aaron.

Understanding the Text

4) What were the two ways people became residents of Jerusalem (verses 1–2)?

_____

_____

_____

_____

_____

_____

5) How did Israel celebrate at the rededication of the walls of Jerusalem (12:27–47)? What part did music and praise play in this ceremony?

_____

_____

_____

_____

_____

_____

(verses to consider: 1 Samuel 4:5; Ezra 3:8–13; Psalm 69:30, 31; Hebrews 13:15)

6) What part did giving (that is, tithes and offerings) play in this time of dedication (12:44–47)?

_____

_____

_____

_____

_____

_____

_____

(verses to consider: 2 Corinthians 8:1–5; 9:7; Philippians 4:18; Hebrews 13:16)

Cross Reference

Read Mark 14:3–9.

³ *And being in Bethany at the house of Simon the leper, as He sat at the table, a woman came having an alabaster flask of very costly oil of spikenard. Then she broke the flask and poured it on His head.*
⁴ *But there were some who were indignant among themselves, and said, "Why was this fragrant oil wasted?*
⁵ *"For it might have been sold for more than three hundred denarii and given to the poor." And they criticized her sharply.*
⁶ *But Jesus said, "Let her alone. Why do you trouble her? She has done a good work for Me.*
⁷ *"For you have the poor with you always, and whenever you wish you may do them good; but Me you do not have always.*
⁸ *"She has done what she could. She has come beforehand to anoint My body for burial.*
⁹ *"Assuredly, I say to you, wherever this gospel is preached in the whole world, what this woman has done will also be told as a memorial to her."*

Exploring the Meaning

7) In what ways is Mary's extravagant and lavish offering a model for all believers?

_____

_____

_____

8) Read Romans 12:1. What does this renowned New Testament passage teach about dedicating oneself to God?

_____

_____

_____

_____

_____

9) Read Psalm 16:11. How is joy inseparable from God?

_____

_____

_____

_____

_____

(verses to consider: Psalm 33:1; Galatians 5:22)

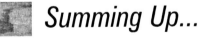

Summing Up...

"Genuine worship is the supreme sacrifice a Christian can offer to Christ. There is a time for ministering to the poor, the sick, the naked, and the imprisoned. There is a time for witnessing to the lost and seeking to lead them to the Savior. There is a time for discipling new believers and helping them grow in the faith. There is a time for careful study and teaching of God's Word. But above all else that the Lord requires of His people is their true worship, without which everything else they may do in His name is empty and powerless."—*John MacArthur*

Reflecting on the Text

10) How do you think the people in your church would respond if the church's leadership asked 10 percent of the congregation to move in order to further God's work? How would you respond?

_____

_____

_____

_____

_____

11) Circle the precise words used to describe the worship of the Israelites at the rededication of the Jerusalem walls (12:27–47). Which of these words are accurate descriptions of your own worship experience of late?

_____

_____

_____

_____

_____

12) Look at your own habits of giving. Are you generous? Would you be embarrassed for your whole church to know the amount of support you have contributed over the last year? Are you a cheerful supporter of the work God wants to do through your own church? What changes do you need to make?

_____

_____

Recording Your Thoughts

For further study, see the following passages:

Deuteronomy 18:1–5	1 Chronicles 23:5	2 Chronicles 29:26
Ezra 3:10	Nehemiah 8:10	Psalm 43:4
Proverbs 16:33	Acts 13:22	

Desperate Times Call for Desperate Measures

Opening Thought

1) In many churches, the pastor often has to take a second job in order to make ends meet. What are the disadvantages of such an arrangement?

_____

_____

_____

_____

2) Do you think Christians should make Sunday a day of rest (similar to the way the Jews rested on the Sabbath)? Why or why not?

_____

_____

_____

_____

3) Does your church practice church discipline? How would the leaders react to a member involved in overt sin? Why is this New Testament command often overlooked by modern congregations?

_____

_____

_____

_____

_____

Background of the Passage

The history of God's people reveals a distressing (if not depressing) truth: heartfelt passion and sincere devotion is often short-lived. Chapter 13 of Nehemiah, the last portion of the Old Testament to be written, is a clear example of this truth.

Nehemiah left Jerusalem in the 32nd year of Artaxerxes, about 433 B.C. (see 5:14; 13:6), and returned to Persia as he had promised (see 2:6). During his absence, the people returned to their former ways, led by the high priest Eliashib (vv. 4, 5). In violation of their earlier promises, they failed to separate themselves from their pagan neighbors. They also failed to support the Levites and priests. A third evidence of their spiritual decline was that they consistently violated the laws of the Sabbath.

It was during Nehemiah's absence that Malachi wrote his prophetic book indicting both priests and people for their sinful defection. Possibly having heard of Eliashib's evil, Nehemiah returned (vv. 4–7) to oversee the needed reforms. His response to the waywardness of the people was swift and severe, reminding us that we must be ruthless in our dealing with sin.

Bible Passage

Read 13:1–31, noting the key words and definitions to the right of the passage.

Nehemiah 13:1–31:
¹ *On that day they read from the Book of Moses in the hearing of the people, and in it was found written that no Ammonite or Moabite should ever come into the assembly of God,*
² *because they had not met the children of Israel with bread and water, but hired Balaam against them to curse them. However, our God turned the curse into a blessing.*
³ *So it was, when they had heard the Law, that they separated all the mixed multitude from Israel.*
⁴ *Now before this, Eliashib the priest, having*

On that day they read from the Book of Moses (vv. 1–2) —Not surprisingly, as they read on the regular calendar cycle, they were confronted with areas in which their thinking and practice had wavered from the Scriptures.

Balaam (v. 2)—see Numbers 22–24

they separated all the mixed multitude (v. 3)—This was done in compliance with their recent pledge (see 10:26–29) before Nehemiah left for Persia.
Tobiah (v. 4)—See note on 2:10.

authority over the storerooms of the house of our God, was allied with Tobiah.

5 And he had prepared for him a large room, where previously they had stored the grain offerings, the frankincense, the articles, the tithes of grain, the new wine and oil, which were commanded to be given to the Levites and singers and gatekeepers, and the offerings for the priests.

6 But during all this I was not in Jerusalem, for in the thirty-second year of Artaxerxes king of Babylon I had returned to the king. Then after certain days I obtained leave from the king,

7 and I came to Jerusalem and discovered the evil that Eliashib had done for Tobiah, in preparing a room for him in the courts of the house of God.

8 And it grieved me bitterly; therefore I threw all the household goods of Tobiah out of the room.

9 Then I commanded them to cleanse the rooms; and I brought back into them the articles of the house of God, with the grain offering and the frankincense.

10 I also realized that the portions for the Levites had not been given them; for each of the Levites and the singers who did the work had gone back to his field.

11 So I contended with the rulers, and said, "Why is the house of God forsaken?" And I gathered them together and set them in their place.

12 Then all Judah brought the tithe of the grain and the new wine and the oil to the storehouse.

13 And I appointed as treasurers over the storehouse Shelemiah the priest and Zadok the scribe, and of the Levites, Pedaiah; and next to them was Hanan the son of Zaccur, the son of Mattaniah; for they were considered faithful, and their task was to distribute to their brethren.

14 Remember me, O my God, concerning this, and do not wipe out my good deeds that I have done for the house of my God, and for its services!

15 In those days I saw people in Judah treading wine presses on the Sabbath, and bringing in sheaves, and loading donkeys with wine, grapes, figs, and all kinds of burdens, which they brought into

Eliashib had allied with Israel's enemy for some personal gain and taken it to such an extreme as to desecrate the house of God.

I had returned to the king (v. 6)—Nehemiah returned to Persia as he promised (see 2:6) about 433 B.C., in the thirty-second year of Artaxerxes (see 5:14). It is unknown exactly how long Nehemiah remained in Persia, perhaps until about 424 B.C., but in that interval the disobedience developed.

it grieved me bitterly (v. 8)—Nehemiah's response to the desecration of the temple was similar to Christ's almost five centuries later.

articles of the house of God (v. 9)—In order to accommodate Tobiah, they had moved the articles of the house of God from their rightful place and put idols in the temple courts.

gone back to his field (v. 10)—By neglecting the tithe, the people failed to support the Levites. Consequently, the Levities had to abandon their responsibilities in the house of God and perform field labor in order to survive.

I contended with the rulers (v. 11)—In Nehemiah's absence, the Jews violated their previous covenant with God regarding offerings (see 10:35–40) as reported by Mal. 1:6–14 and 3:8–12. In his presence, it was immediately restored (see notes on 9:38–10:39).

Remember me (v. 14)—This refrain is used three times here, once after each rebuke (see 13:22, 31).

on the Sabbath (v. 15)—They went against their previous

Jerusalem on the Sabbath day. And I warned them about the day on which they were selling provisions.

16 Men of Tyre dwelt there also, who brought in fish and all kinds of goods, and sold them on the Sabbath to the children of Judah, and in Jerusalem.

17 Then I contended with the nobles of Judah, and said to them, "What evil thing is this that you do, by which you profane the Sabbath day?

18 "Did not your fathers do thus, and did not our God bring all this disaster on us and on this city? Yet you bring added wrath on Israel by profaning the Sabbath."

19 So it was, at the gates of Jerusalem, as it began to be dark before the Sabbath, that I commanded the gates to be shut, and charged that they must not be opened till after the Sabbath. Then I posted some of my servants at the gates, so that no burdens would be brought in on the Sabbath day.

20 Now the merchants and sellers of all kinds of wares lodged outside Jerusalem once or twice.

21 Then I warned them, and said to them, "Why do you spend the night around the wall? If you do so again, I will lay hands on you!" From that time on they came no more on the Sabbath.

22 And I commanded the Levites that they should cleanse themselves, and that they should go and guard the gates, to sanctify the Sabbath day. Remember me, O my God, concerning this also, and spare me according to the greatness of Your mercy!

23 In those days I also saw Jews who had married women of Ashdod, Ammon, and Moab.

24 And half of their children spoke the language of Ashdod, and could not speak the language of Judah, but spoke according to the language of one or the other people.

25 So I contended with them and cursed them, struck some of them and pulled out their hair, and made them swear by God, saying, "You shall not give your daughters as wives to their sons, nor take their daughters for your sons or yourselves.

covenant by violating the Sabbath (see 10:31).

Tyre (v. 16)—a Phoenician coastal town 20 miles south of Sidon

you bring added wrath on Israel by profaning the Sabbath (v. 18)—Jeremiah had rebuked their fathers for the same things (see Jer. 17:21–27). By such acts their fathers had brought the misery of exile and oppression, and they were doing the same—increasing God's wrath against them.

I will lay hands on you (v. 21) —Nehemiah had to force compliance with threats.

Ashdod (v. 23)—see note on 4:7

Ammon, and Moab (v. 23)— neighboring countries east of the Jordan whose beginnings were by Lot's incestuous relationship with his two daughters (see Gen. 19:30–38)

²⁶ *"Did not Solomon king of Israel sin by these things? Yet among many nations there was no king like him, who was beloved of his God; and God made him king over all Israel. Nevertheless pagan women caused even him to sin.*

²⁷ *"Should we then hear of your doing all this great evil, transgressing against our God by marrying pagan women?"*

²⁸ *And one of the sons of Joiada, the son of Eliashib the high priest, was a son-in-law of Sanballat the Horonite; therefore I drove him from me.*

²⁹ *Remember them, O my God, because they have defiled the priesthood and the covenant of the priesthood and the Levites.*

³⁰ *Thus I cleansed them of everything pagan. I also assigned duties to the priests and the Levites, each to his service,*

³¹ *and to bringing the wood offering and the first-fruits at appointed times.*
Remember me, O my God, for good!

this great evil (v. 27)—Both the priests and the people had married pagans of the land in violation of the Mosaic law (see Ex. 34:15, 16; Deut. 7:3), the earlier reforms of Ezra (see Ezra 9, 10), and their own covenant (see 10:30). Malachi spoke against this sin (Mal. 2:10–16).

one of the sons of Joiada (v. 28)—Even the grandson of the high priest (see 12:10) sinfully married a daughter of Sanballat (see note on 2:10).

Remember me (v. 31)— Nehemiah prayed this for the third time (see 13:14, 22), desiring God's blessing on his obedient efforts.

Understanding the Text

4) What did the Israelites discover when they read the Book of Moses at the celebration, and how did they respond (13:1—3)?

_____

_____

5) What evil deed did Eliashib do and how did Nehemiah respond?

_____

_____

6) What turn of events had forced the Levites to work in the fields? (13:10)

_____

_____

7) What did Nehemiah do in light of the Israelites' failure to keep the Sabbath holy (vv. 19–22)?

_____

_____

(verses to consider: Exodus 20:8; 34:21; Jeremiah 17:21–27)

Cross Reference

Read 1 Kings 11:1–11.

1 *But King Solomon loved many foreign women, as well as the daughter of Pharaoh: women of the Moabites, Ammonites, Edomites, Sidonians, and Hittites—*

2 *from the nations of whom the LORD had said to the children of Israel, "You shall not intermarry with them, nor they with you. Surely they will turn away your hearts after their gods." Solomon clung to these in love.*

3 *And he had seven hundred wives, princesses, and three hundred concubines; and his wives turned away his heart.*

4 *For it was so, when Solomon was old, that his wives turned his heart after other gods; and his heart was not loyal to the LORD his God, as was the heart of his father David.*

5 *For Solomon went after Ashtoreth the goddess of the Sidonians, and after Milcom the abomination of the Ammonites.*

6 *Solomon did evil in the sight of the LORD, and did not fully follow the LORD, as did his father David.*

7 *Then Solomon built a high place for Chemosh the abomination of Moab, on the hill that is east of Jerusalem, and for Molech the abomination of the people of Ammon.*

8 *And he did likewise for all his foreign wives, who burned incense and sacrificed to their gods.*

9 *So the LORD became angry with Solomon, because his heart had turned from the LORD God of Israel, who had appeared to him twice,*

10 *and had commanded him concerning this thing, that he should not go after other gods; but he did not keep what the LORD had commanded.*

11 *Therefore the LORD said to Solomon, "Because you have done this, and have not kept My covenant and My statutes, which I have commanded you, I will surely tear the kingdom away from you and give it to your servant.*

Exploring the Meaning

8) How should the example of Solomon have discouraged the Jews in Nehemiah's time from marrying foreign wives?

_____

_____

(verses to consider: 2 Corinthians 6:14–18)

9) Read Matthew 21:12. How did Nehemiah's grief over the desecration of the temple resemble Christ's some 400 years later?

_____

_____

(verses to consider: Isaiah 56:7; Jeremiah 7:11; John 2:13–17).

10) Read Malachi 2:1–8. Does God hold ministers to a higher standard? If so, in what way?

_____

_____

(verses to consider: Matthew 23:1–36)

Summing Up...

"Every kind of sin, from disorderly conduct to immorality to false teaching, is to be disciplined. And all Christians, from the newest believer to the most experienced leader, are subject to that discipline. To be spiritually healthy and effective in its ministry the church must deal with sin within its own ranks. To trifle with sin, to ignore it under the guise of love, or to fail for any other reason to cleanse the church of it is disastrous."—_John MacArthur_

Reflecting on the Text

11) General William Booth, founder of the Salvation Army, once told a group

of new officers: "I want you young men always to bear in mind that it is the nature of a fire to go out; you must keep it stirred and fed and the ashes removed."

On a scale of 1–10 (with 1 being "dying embers" and 10 being "white hot coals") what is your spiritual temperature right now?

_____

_____

12) Nehemiah discovered Tobiah, an enemy of the Jews, living in the temple complex! What sinful attitudes or actions have you allowed in your life?

_____

_____

13) How have close associations with people of the world had a negative effect on your spiritual health?

_____

_____

14) In what way can you renew your commitment to the priority of worship?

_____

_____

Recording Your Thoughts

_____

_____

_____

For further study, see the following passages:

Genesis 19:30–38	Exodus 12:38	Leviticus 21:14
Numbers 11:4–6	Deuteronomy 12:19	Deuteronomy 23:3–6
Ezra 9:3	1 Corinthians 4:2	1 John 4:5–6

The MacArthur Bible Collection

John MacArthur, General Editor

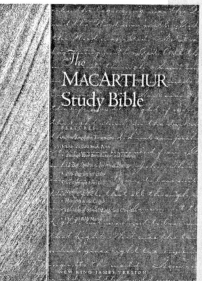

The MacArthur Study Bible

From the moment you pick it up, you'll know it's a classic. Featuring the word-for-word accuracy of the New King James Version, *The MacArthur Study Bible* is perfect for serious study. Pastor/teacher John MacArthur has compiled more than 20,000 study notes, a 200-page topical index and numerous charts, maps, outlines, and articles to create *The MacArthur Study Bible*. This Bible has been crafted with the finest materials in a variety of handsome bindings, including hardcover and indexed bonded leather. Winner of "The 1998 Study Bible of the Year Award."

The MacArthur Topical Bible

In the excellent tradition of *Nave's Topical Bible,* this newly created reference book incorporates thousands of topics and ideas, both traditional and contemporary, for believers today and in the new millennium. Carefully researched and prepared by Dr. John MacArthur and the faculty of Masters Seminary, *The MacArthur Topical Bible* will quickly become the reference of choice of all serious Bible students. Using the New King James translation, this Bible is arranged alphabetically by topic and is completely cross-referenced. This exhaustive resource is an indispensible tool for the topical study of God's Word.

The MacArthur Bible Studies

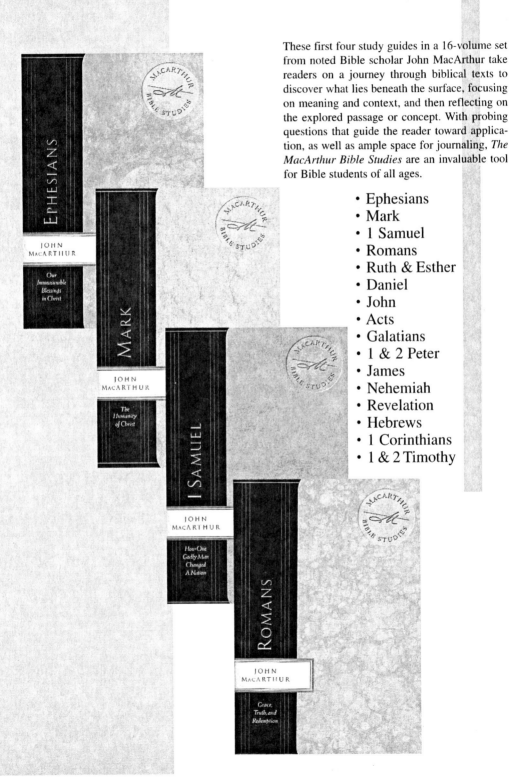

These first four study guides in a 16-volume set from noted Bible scholar John MacArthur take readers on a journey through biblical texts to discover what lies beneath the surface, focusing on meaning and context, and then reflecting on the explored passage or concept. With probing questions that guide the reader toward application, as well as ample space for journaling, *The MacArthur Bible Studies* are an invaluable tool for Bible students of all ages.

- Ephesians
- Mark
- 1 Samuel
- Romans
- Ruth & Esther
- Daniel
- John
- Acts
- Galatians
- 1 & 2 Peter
- James
- Nehemiah
- Revelation
- Hebrews
- 1 Corinthians
- 1 & 2 Timothy